The Tender Heart of Sadness

28 Aspects of Warriorship Drawn from the Buddhist and Shambhala Traditions

To Nicole!
Ki Ki So So!
Best wishes

1/15/10

The Tender Heart of Sadness

28 Aspects of Warriorship Drawn from the Buddhist and Shambhala Traditions

ROGER GUEST

With a preface by
Acharya Suzann Duquette

Aventine Press

Published by Aventine Press
750 State St. #319
San Diego CA, 92101
www.aventinepress.com

ISBN: 1-59330-620-2

THIS BOOK IS DEDICATED TO

The Master Warrior known to the world as
The Dorje Dradul of Mukpo,
The Profound, Brilliant, Just, Powerful,
All-Victorious Druk Sakyong,
Vidyadhara, the Venerable Chogyam Trungpa Rinpoche

And to his son and lineage heir,
Sakyong Mipham Rinpoche,

And to my own sons,
Xavier and Jefferson

Acknowledgments

Writing this book has been a long, edifying and richly rewarding journey that has taken me to places I might never have otherwise gone. As a result, I will be forever grateful to those countless friends, family and acquaintances who have offered their time, assistance, critical insight, guidance, food, shelter, encouragement and discouragement along the way.

My travelling party has included a host of friends, editors, critics and cynics. Hopefully, you know who you are and that I am deeply grateful to all of you. However, I must single out my primary editor, Michelle Cox, whose quiet dedication, perseverance and attention to detail turned out to be the perfect tonic for my gin. It has been a joy to work with someone of such integrity, skill, patience, tolerance, flexibility and effervescence.

Special appreciation also goes out to Acharyas Pema Chodron, Richard John and Suzann Duquette for their encouragement and advice. Also Noni Regan, Bethany Perron, Michael Carroll, Christine Baranay, John and Tracy Suchocki, Dean and Jaynine Nelson, and Barry Rossinoff, who have continued to provide friendship and support through this process. My larger thank-you list includes at least another hundred names and rather than risk painful omissions, I intend to thank each and every one of you personally when we meet again. I must, however, express particular gratitude to my sister, Christine Guest, who kindly offered the cover photograph and James Wagner for his help in putting it together.

My deepest bow goes to my karmic companion, Molly Kluss, whose love, interest and insights laid waste to my defenses and propelled me forward.

From the beginning, this book was intended as a tribute to my guru, the late Dorje Dradul of Mukpo, the venerable Chogyam Trungpa Rinpoche, and to his son, the glorious Sakyong Mipham Rinpoche, whose brilliance continues to illuminate our world. Although it falls short of doing their teachings justice, I turn to them and to all my fellow warriors with a lifelong sense of gratitude. I pray that those who aspire to embody the message of basic goodness everywhere, whether according to the glorious Tiger Lion Garuda Dragon tradition of Shambhala, or any other truly authentic tradition, are filled with lungta and the blessings of a stainless lineage. May we encourage each other for the good of all! May the Great Eastern Sun be victorious!

Foreword

Roger has shared this book with me – a chapter here, a chapter there – over the past few years. Each time, I was amazed at his delightful and penetrating style and how he inspired me to slow down, open up, and extend my sense perceptions. The following pages are about love, relaxation, mindfulness, how to live, and how to die. They offer sound advice on awakening with heart while embracing being human.

I first met Roger Guest in the mid-1970s, sharing a ride to a meditation program led by Chögyam Trungpa Rinpoche. Along the way, we talked about meditation practice. Roger had already been practicing sitting meditation for a few years then, and he's been practicing and teaching meditation ever since.

Roger has a way with words. This, coupled with humanity and a depth of practice, translates into a remarkable ability to unlock complex concepts and penetrate the heart. *The Tender Heart of Sadness* reflects Roger's wonderful talents. In it, he reveals essential teachings on how we can awaken to our inherent wisdom and engage the world in which we live.

These are taxing times – economically, physically, socially, and spiritually. We are in the midst of tremendous speed, aggression, prejudice, anxiety, greed, and potential devastation of the planet. Illness and hunger abound unnecessarily. In these times, kindness and compassion sound mushy, and virtue sounds almost archaic. Buddhist teachings call this time a Dark Age.

These times require teachings that penetrate the thick skin of "me" and motivate us to look closely at our minds and hearts to see what is important. If we aspire to help ourselves and others now and in the future, we must find and maintain our motivation and discover what we can do that is of most benefit. To unblock the power of awareness, we need guidance and a pathway. As Roger says in Chapter 6:

> *Relaxing into the present moment can reconnect us to our intrinsic sanity, and raising our gazes with awareness can open our hearts. We need to look at the world with open eyes, not cower and shut down. Unless what we see, hear, smell or touch actually penetrates our hearts, we will just go through the motions. If meditation takes root, as it could, it is possible that we will rediscover how to kindle the flames of insight so that a whole new crop of human beings will be able to harness their inherent enlightenment.*

In *The Tender Heart of Sadness*, Roger has chosen pivotal topics of the Shambhala Buddhist tradition that describe the very essence of meditation and how it can help us live authentic, awake, and heart-filled lives. Through poetic language, stories, examples, and his wicked sense of humor, Roger brings us teachings on attention, emotions, humbleness, fearlessness, and nowness, all within a context of warriorship – not being afraid of who we are and a willingness to engage our life as it is. These are topics to chew on, which make us want to practice and learn more. Sprinkled throughout the book are short contemplations and meditation practices that help us to feel what is being said, to soak in the meaning of the words.

Of course, to really soak in these teachings and apply them, we need to be willing to change. This book offers key points to guide us in that direction. It reads like a page-turner while offering life-changing advice. From Chapter 12:

The greatest breakthroughs happen when we venture outside the orbit of our egos. We transcend ego-striving only to surrender to a truth that is larger than our own, something we might call the 'Big Picture'.

My wish is that *The Tender Heart of Sadness* will expand your mind and heart to a 'big picture' journey of spiritual growth and joy that has the power to change the world.

Acharya Suzann Duquette
Barnet, Vermont

Table of Contents

Introduction

In the summer of 1974, at the age of 22, I was a young man primed for life and spiritual adventure. I had just returned to my native British Columbia after extensive travels through Europe, North Africa and Asia: a journey which had profoundly altered my view of life. I had worked on a sailboat in Portugal, planted avocados in the Canary Islands and herded cows in Switzerland. Essentially, I was circumambulating the globe on a shoestring when I landed in a small rural monastery outside Katmandu, Nepal, and met and fell in love with Tibetan Buddhism. Unfortunately, feeling both inspired and forlorn, I ran out of money in the middle of the honeymoon and was forced to return home.

It was hard to leave and I missed the East before my feet hit North American soil. One part of me wanted to immediately raise the funds to return to Nepal and become a monk, another part was more cautious. Since adolescence I had known that my spiritual needs were not going to be met in the sleepy theism of middle class America. I also knew that I couldn't commit myself to a life of simply making money, acquiring 'stuff' and 'getting ahead.' I craved the intimate relationship with reality that meditation promised and, after my encounters in Asia, I knew I had to keep moving forward. So, an auspicious combination of youthful spirit, inquisitiveness and good luck attracted me to a young charismatic Tibetan teacher by the name of Chogyam Trungpa Rinpoche. Word had spread that in Boulder, Colorado he had recently founded a school called Naropa Institute. Still brimming with my newfound devotion for Buddhadharma, I accepted the invitation of a friend and set off to enroll.

The man I was destined to meet had a far more compelling story than my own. While still in his late teens, he had been enthroned as the abbot of an influential monastery only to find himself in the crosshairs of Mao Tse Tung's advancing army. In that remote region of Eastern Tibet, beyond the purview of television cameras or newspaper reporters, ancient monasteries were being leveled, monks tortured and killed, and the local population terrorized by systematic genocide. Despite his age, people looked to Trungpa Rinpoche for leadership. So, on the advice of his teachers and with very little time to prepare, he gathered a small heroic band of monks and locals and set off on a treacherous escape over the highest mountains on earth, eventually to the safety of India.

It is hard to imagine a more painful or challenging situation. Yet, amidst chaos and utter devastation, he was able to glimpse the larger picture. He saw that the communists, in their vain efforts to destroy Tibet, were unintentionally forcing open the treasure vault of wisdom and compassion known as Tibetan Buddhism. Still, as he turned to leave behind a culture steeped in centuries of enlightenment, and enter another, which was just finding its footing after the trauma of world war, this young exiled prince could not possibly have known the pivotal role that he would play in the profound historic developments that would follow.

The wild and circuitous route that brought Rinpoche to North America in 1970 was fraught with obstacles. Along the way, he suffered a debilitating car accident, shed his monk's robes, fathered a child, published his first book (*Meditation in Action*) and took a young British bride. Even so, within a few months of his arrival in Montreal, he and a ragtag group of eager hippies arranged to purchase a rundown farm in Barnet, Vermont. Almost immediately, rumors spread of a cool, young Tibetan lama teaching Buddhism and meditation on a commune in the Northeast Kingdom. Students and dilettantes alike flocked from far and wide. Before long, this humble community of poets, curiosity seekers, intellectuals and misfits evolved into a disciplined contemplative community which they called Tail of the Tiger. Now known as Karmê Chöling, it ranks among the most respected Buddhist practice centers in the western hemisphere.

By 1974, Rinpoche's presence on the spiritual scene was still gathering momentum. He had published his second book, a groundbreaking best-seller entitled *Cutting Through Spiritual Materialism,* and was attracting respectful audiences everywhere he spoke. Clusters of eager students had begun forming urban practice centers across the USA and Canada. When the suggestion arose of bringing together artists, poets, musicians, creative dancers, yogis, Zen masters, and other spiritual teachers for a summer of contemplation and celebration, Rinpoche was all for it. And so, against the backdrop of Watergate and nuclear protests, Naropa Institute took birth in Boulder, Colorado that summer of 1974.

My first meeting with Rinpoche was an awkward, almost comical affair. Auspiciously, on my way to Colorado, I heard that the Venerable Kalu Rinpoche and some other high lamas were offering three days of empowerments in Vancouver and I was eager to attend. It later became obvious that, like many of my cohorts, I was prone to confusing the mere receiving of profound teachings and blessings with the actual realization of them. As would later be pointed out, by emphasizing the forms while not fully engaging in the practices, I was actually reinforcing my ego. Thus, I arrived in Boulder somewhat confused and in need of guidance, genuinely open to any insight Trungpa Rinpoche might offer. I am sure I secretly conjectured that a few clever questions or comments might reveal some 'specialness' on my part.

After attending my first talk, I remember being both baffled and utterly spellbound. In those days, Rinpoche wore western clothes, smoked cigarettes and lingered on the stage after his lectures to meet individually with those who had questions. So that evening when the usual line formed, I was there. At my turn, I launched into my story, emphasizing how I had been in such and such a place and studied with this or that lama and how I had received this and that empowerment and so on. Midway through my pathetic monologue, Rinpoche stopped me and stated kindly, yet with authority, "I think you should sit!", "Forget all the rest of it for now and just sit!" In that moment, I became his student.

HIDDEN TREASURE

Fast forward to the winter of 1976. While directing a three-month seminary in Land of Lakes, Wisconsin, Rinpoche began making references to something called the "Great Eastern Sun". This new term was accompanied by a shift in his tone and a subtle, but distinctly different, air: a sense that something significant yet mysterious was happening. Despite our confusion, Rinpoche's excitement was invigorating and contagious. Little did we know, but the Shambhala teachings were being presented on American soil for the first time.

It turned out that Rinpoche, himself, was receiving teachings in the form of a 'terma' or "hidden treasure" transmission. Around this time, as the story goes, he would sit at a table, pick up a pen and begin writing in Tibetan as if taking dictation from a source beyond thought. He later identified his inspiration as the Rigdens of Shambhala. When a great teacher (terton) receives terma teachings, he or she understands their meaning directly but does not claim authorship in the traditional sense. In this case, Rinpoche, guided by what would become known as the vision of the Great Eastern Sun, accepted the responsibility to protect and propagate a body of sacred wisdom that formed the basis of a path of practices and study called Shambhala Training.

The word *Shambhala*, and the images the term elicits, were in no way a cavalier invention of Trungpa Rinpoche. Throughout Asia, tales of the ancient Kingdom of Shambhala had long formed a cherished living legend. Shambhala is more real to the average Tibetan than Camelot is to the average Englishman. It has deep, esoteric roots that extend far into the cultural and social fabric of the entire Himalayan region.

Knowing only that we trusted Rinpoche, whenever he chose to introduce new material, we listened. On the surface, these fresh teachings did not seem to differ radically from the advanced Buddhist path he had previously presented. However, as we listened more closely, it became clear that there was a profound twist and some kind of transcendental method to his madness. The Shambhala teachings, we soon discovered, with their focus on fearlessness, gentleness, dignity and warriorship, challenged us to look at our world through a powerful new lens.

Since Buddhism's arrival in Tibet around the eighth century, it has spawned thousands, if not tens of thousands, of enlightened teachers. Among them were a handful of extraordinary beings who displayed prophetic powers and foretold of a coming dark age. They warned of a time when the glory of the Buddhist teachings would be overshadowed by negativity and materialistic insanity. Their writings suggested that not only would the glory of Tibet, the land of snows, experience attacks of devastating suffering and darkness, but also that the whole world would be thrust into a period of sinister despair. One example of such prophecy is expressed in the following brief excerpt from a chant written in the early nineteenth century. While ancient predictions did not force his hand, Trungpa Rinpoche had us recite this chant at specifically dark times of the year.

> ... *"When sons do not listen to their fathers' words,*
> *An evil time when relatives quarrel*
> *When people dress sloppily in clothes of rags,*
> *Eating bad cheap food,*
> *When there are family feuds and civil wars,*
> *This provokes the Black Mamos*' wrath.*
>
> *The sky is thick with purple clouds of sickness.*
> *They incite cosmic warfare,*
> *They destroy by causing the age of weaponry.*
> *Suddenly they strike men with fatal ulcerous sores...*

Trungpa Rinpoche saw a world in great peril in need of spiritual and social leadership. He viewed fundamental human nature as basically good and championed the proclamation of human dignity. Yet, he knew that a society fixated on immediate gratification and blind to the devastating impact of its shortsighted actions was on a slippery slope. He taught that if Buddhism is the sun, or Christianity or Hinduism or any genuine wisdom tradition is the sun, Shambhala is the clear sky in which that sun can shine. He encouraged us to re-examine our basic relationships with reality and to embrace the sacredness of the world by rekindling our appreciation of the most ordinary aspects of everyday existence. How we spoke, how we ate, where we slept and what we read- everything mattered! And everything continues to matter. Accordingly, the Shambhala teachings were offered as a template for an enlightened society.

THE AWAKENED WARRIOR

Warriorship is not a casual walk in the park; it is a path of fearless dignity. Unfortunately, many well-intended but ill-fated spiritual or philosophical expeditions never discover the real root of human despair or conquer the summits of spiritual realization. On one hand, those who have succeeded on this journey have left behind clear instructions- not to fear our true natures. On the other hand, they have entreated us to be vigilant in avoiding the "*slime and muck of the dark age.*" If we can open our hearts and embrace the present moment, we are taught, the vision of an enlightened society can be realized. If our goal is merely to be revered or to win intellectual debates, the false promises and deceptive trappings of spiritual materialism will easily seduce us into depravity. There will always be charlatans ready to promise us salvation through flashy demonstrations of faith and ideological trickery. But particularly at this time, we cannot afford to squander our precious spiritual resources. The stakes are simply too high.

Shambhala warriorship puts us in touch with ourselves and encourages us to be brave, awake and attentive to others. As we work with our depression, laziness and deceit, we must also be aware of the sunrise of genuine goodness that is evident in every moment. The warrior aspires to live in the fresh air of sanity, on the spot, where the concept of taking time off is meaningless. While this attitude may sound lofty and idealistic, warriorship challenges our assumptions and forces us to deprogram ourselves from the core addictions of ego. In this sense, freeing the mind to live fully in the moment is the warrior's mission.

We are all subject to powerful forces in nature that would have us turn our backs on our inner dignity. Yet, giving in to doubts about our own basic goodness leads us away from the vividness of presence. This denial of brilliance is what Trungpa Rinpoche called the *Setting Sun* mentality of ego. This inclination lies in stark contrast to the *Great Eastern Sun* vision, or a genuine warrior's outlook. It could be said that even in a world of pain and sadness, the warrior dares to dream the dream of enlightenment. This does not mean we live in some fantasy of the future, but that we have the courage and conviction to be fully present, open hearted, and engaged in every moment.

Setting Sun mind is claustrophobic by nature. Nobody thrives in the stale air of cowardice, curled up in a cocoon of habitual patterns. It is natural to hunger for the original freshness of life; for fresh air, fresh food, fresh water and fresh ideas. Even if we seem hopelessly addicted to cheap comforts and old emotional patterns, there comes a time when we have to get up off the couch, recharge our batteries and regain our zest. Because basic goodness is everyone's fundamental nature, the seeds of dignity are ready to sprout and grow in every heart, given the right conditions.

Shambhala warriorship restores the cowardly mind of fear to a state of unconditional confidence. The emerging warrior is inspired to meet the world in all its pain and glory and to extend real wakefulness into every activity, whether secular or spiritual. We are not just trying to have a better life; simply emerging from neurosis for ourselves alone is not quite enough. The Great Eastern Sun shines the light of elegance, fearlessness and care into every aspect of our lives with far reaching and profound implications.

My love affair with Tibetan Buddhism that began back in 1974 has endured and broadened to include these Shambhala teachings. What my parents once expected to be a whimsical infatuation has, in my opinion, proved to be a very fruitful marriage. During the thirteen years that I spent with my teacher, I studied Buddhism and the Shambhala teachings side by side. I encourage others to do the same. I have remained an active teacher in both the Shambhala and Buddhist traditions and expect to continue to deepen my understanding and practice by working with the current lineage holder, Trungpa Rinpoche's son, Sakyong Mipham Rinpoche, as well as with other authentic teachers, as long as I live.

Today, we are serenaded by a chorus of many wonderful voices, including new masters who have arisen from both inside and outside the Buddhist and Shambhalian worlds. As they sing the message of nowness in fresh languages and with renewed vigor, I feel hopeful. May they continue to clearly echo and amplify the profound beat of the Shambhala warrior's drum and join the dance with tender hearts of genuine sadness! And, in that spirit, may this small offering be of some benefit.

1. Back to Square One

Normally, when we walk we don't think about walking, we think about where we are going. In meditation we forget where we are going and return to the walking.

All human beings, regardless of age, history or expertise, share an instinctual desire for inner peace. Surely, if true and lasting serenity could be assured in one physical location, we'd all be scrambling to get there. Likewise, if there were a safe drug or elixir that could produce lasting enlightenment without any negative side effects, we'd all be enlightened by now. However, we can't afford to waste our time in wishful thinking or searching for some easy way out. Life is short and we have been fooled too many times. Since ignorance arises in the mind, it must be dealt with by the mind, and the only time we may ever have to work on our minds is right now.

The fact that we suffer does not make us 'bad' people. Nor can we be faulted for desiring a dependable and stable reality, a sanctuary away from the stresses of the world or even a reasonable psychological escape from the suffering that pervades our lives. Sometimes we look to particular teachers, therapists or exceptional friends to anchor or soothe our troubled minds. We may have particular places we like to go to gain a clearer perspective, and sometimes, we simply zone out. However, when we lose our connection to reality, we lose a degree of consciousness and are often disoriented. And because we are confused, we tend to make poor decisions. Therefore, it is essential to find a trustworthy port within the chaos of our own experience where we can continually plug back into the energy of basic awareness. Fortunately, such connections exist.

Based on the profound counsel of enlightened meditators of the past and present, our most trustworthy refuge is the present moment. Whatever it is that is affecting our minds, we can never improve on being awake to the present moment, this very moment, right now. The clearest answers to life's ultimate questions are always found in the immediacy of experience.

Feelings of inadequacy and doubt may have always been part of our life experience, but they do not have to be. Usually, we believe that if we had just one more powerful technique or one more slightly advanced or streamlined method, the secrets to a perfect existence would be ours. But that line of reasoning has its limits. Imprisonment and freedom are always a matter of presence. The game of questions and answers, at some point, is just another way of keeping ourselves occupied and conveniently distracted from the direct experience of this moment.

So sitting still and just relating with where we are right now, as it turns out, is best. Rather than pursuing an exotic and complicated path, our ordinary breath becomes the cardinal point on our spiritual compass. When we're lost in the neurotic jungle, the one footprint we can always trust is our breath. Simply relating to the nowness of inhalation or exhalation can reorient our awareness. When we bring our attention back to the breath, instead of being lost in thought, we're back on the path.

A corpse doesn't breathe. The feeling of air passing through our nostrils indicates that we're alive, and if that is all we have going for us, that's a good start. Finding one breath is actually a great beginning. The sense of well-being associated with the expansion and deflation of our lungs is probably the most basic and most reassuring psychic sign of survival known to mankind. When a healthy consciousness notices the breath going in and out, it is like a thread that sews the mind and body together. No other reference point gives life the same wholesome sense of continuity.

We breathe regardless of what we happen to be doing, thinking, feeling, hearing or seeing. No matter how tired, refreshed, excited, tormented or bored we may be, we cannot take time off from breathing. From birth to death, each breath may be virtually indistinguishable from the last, and perhaps nothing could be more boring; but at the same time, what could be more fulfilling? Only when we become fully alert to the process of inhaling and exhaling, do we tune into the process of living. As our nostrils fill with oxygen, we taste our own presence, the exquisite sense of being alive. Following the trail of each exhalation, we discover places words cannot describe. Passing through the jungle of thought, we arrive again at a clearing, that cosmic intersection of the here and now that forms a gap between the past and the future. And from that vantage point we regain our ultimate bearings.

Perhaps we envision the self to be a fortress-like identity that never changes. Maybe we fantasize a time when all our problems will be solved, once and for all and we can live happily ever after in a state of peace, free of our irritating and ubiquitous inner voices and that nagging sense of ME! The ecumenical notion of networks of yellow-brick roads all leading to the same spiritual Oz has its conceptual appeal. But we can't afford to waste time on spiritual sidetracks; too often, we lose track of the real destination of our efforts and even the path feels too slippery to pin down. After a while, we may have to admit that we are lost. At such junctures, we have to return to the breath because it is the only reference point with any grip on time and space, simply because it only happens right here and right now.

Although its sheer immediacy makes it hard to map, this present moment is what we call "Square One". As the nexus where mind and breath come together, Square One simultaneously marks the birthplace and tombstone of ego, as well as the fountain of form and emptiness. Only at Square One can we gain a tangible sense of wholesomeness and dignity. No matter how far the wandering mind travels, nowhere else can it assume the natural seat of awakened consciousness. Square One is mind's ultimate destination. We can search the vast expanse of the universe for a more welcoming, more wondrous home, only to come up short every time. Trungpa Rinpoche used to speak of 'the reference point of no reference point', which can never be improved upon. Square One, the illusive gap of nowness, is that primordial dot at the center of the metaphysical universe. Every time we awaken from the dream of time we find ourselves back at Square One. If a lightening bolt of direct experience strikes us, guess where it hits.

When endless excursions into the realm of thought fall flat, we return to the breath by default. In this way, Square One moves beneath our feet like our shadow, making the journey itself the destination. Groping around in the jungle of discursiveness is exhausting, until eventually, there is no choice but to surrender to simplicity. In the end, nothing else works; our primordial confidence in the power of our own presence distracts us from our distractions.

Mindful breathing establishes a conscious relationship with the universe that allows us to genuinely extend our compassion to the world. A present-minded focus generates strength because we see others clearly. We can afford to shoulder their struggles because our own egos are dissolving. Eventually, life becomes a journey without beginning or end, joyously dedicated to the welfare of all beings.

In walking meditation, awareness shifts from the breath to the feet. We move forward physically but we never leave the present moment; we simply take one step at a time. Normally, when we walk we don't think about walking, we think about where we are going. In meditation, we forget where we are going and return to the walking. In so doing, a sense of stillness starts to pervade all motion. The feeling of one foot touching the ground as the other foot lifts, moves, and again touches down, highlights the freshness of simultaneously arriving and letting go. No matter how slowly or quickly we walk, we cannot escape nowness. By placing our awareness on the act of walking, we relate to our physical presence and our psychological presence at the same time. Proceeding from breath to breath and step to step, we say goodbye to the past and the future, and say hello again and again to Square One.

Warriors not only appreciate the magic relationship between the mind and the breath, they master it. These days, with the traumas of life erupting all around us, it is important not to be intimidated by the pace and turbulence of outer events. As a good friend puts it, "Every moment is an unfolding, like continually unwrapping a gift. Just look at all the wonderful and surprising things that have already happened today!"

The path of warriorship leads us out of the tragic and into the magic. By applying the genuine spiritual alchemy of mindfulness, we take the raw, rugged qualities of mind and refine them into real gold. Uncertainty, fear and aggression are transformed into confidence, gentleness and fearlessness. Eventually, every second of existence is polished by an outlook of sacredness so that it sparkles with freshness and radiates the brilliance of presence.

2. Attention

The ultimate gift that one human being can offer another is pure, undistracted attention.

A cat walks into the room. It pounces onto the bed where a young woman is studying. She picks it up with one hand and briefly looking up from her notes, pets it with the other. She then lifts the small animal to her face, looks into its eyes, rubs noses and gently tosses it back to the floor. The cat retreats to the hallway and the woman returns to her notes. For the moment, both have been fed.

Like that cat, any one of us might find ourselves prowling the halls vying for attention. We, too, instinctively purr when we're happy and moan when we're in pain. Like all beings, we carry the subtle burden of loneliness and generate unique shadows to fit our forms. Seemingly in order to confirm our existence, we seek out encounters with one another. Like groundhogs, we gather our resolve amidst our insecurities and pick a moment to ascend from our burrows and check out the world. Sometimes, we see our outlines in the snow, sometimes we don't. And when we fail to find the confirmation we seek, we quietly slip back down our holes only to try again another day.

Somehow in the light of each other's attentiveness, our basic anxieties and sanities are highlighted. Whenever two people approach one another, subtle forms of energy are exchanged. Delicate sparks of electricity arc across space. In a simple handshake we transmit and receive all kinds of information. When we kiss, our lips are like two wires completing a circuit allowing us to taste each other's aliveness. When we look into each other's eyes, we see ourselves reflected in the living mirror of another mind.

We are social creatures. Since our first ancestors noticed that a gaze could be returned, attention has been the universal currency in the marketplace of *interbeing*. The unquenchable human thirst for companionship has enhanced and given meaning to our lives. The hum of messages crossing the great divide between giver and receiver, observer and observed, lover and beloved has kept the motor of humanity buzzing. It is impossible to conceive of life without the intercourse of attention. We would have no emotional energy to stir the great metaphysical soup and no enthusiasm to share mutual nourishment or draw out the poetry and flavors of each other's hearts. Attention is the blood of communication and realization. The more genuine and intimate we are with one another, the more we learn about ourselves.

The ultimate gift that one human being can offer another is pure, undistracted attention. From a very early age, we learn that simple naive attention is valued even when we have nothing to offer but a smile. Attention has a primordial power that we fashion into a tool for survival. By withholding it here, or using it as a seductive lure there, we learn to manipulate our infantile cosmos. Much later, we realize that others are willing to pay for our attention. We agree to provide it to an employer for a price, recognizing that with attention comes the inherent promise of productivity. Embedded in the deal is the notion of self-worth which is quantified as a wage. If the price assigned to our attention is undervalued or inflated, we feel uneasy. Likewise, when our attention wanders too far from the assigned task, we feel as if we're cheating.

From an early age, warriors train themselves to harness attention. I remember playing a childhood game of hide and seek in a pitch-black corner of a friend's basement and trying hard to remain perfectly still in a dark nook. As my friend approached, I remember inhaling and exhaling very quietly and slowly, so as not to alert him to my whereabouts, and having the distinct sensation that my thoughts were too loud. But how can you think more quietly? My friend was literally two feet away from my face. How could he not hear the thunderous drum of my heartbeat? Even the molecules in the air seemed energized as he passed by without seeing me.

When that spark of recognition leaps across the gap, a flood gate opens. We cannot help but be curious about who lives behind another's eyes and whether the owner of such red lips has the same experience of red that we do. We long to be entangled in the enigma of intimacy and play in the crossfire of passion and inquisitiveness. As my outgoing attention meets your incoming attention, the confluence creates a silent whirlpool of life looking back at life. Energy floods the existential hollows of our beings and, like a breeze feathering across the surface of an emotional pond, our aliveness shimmers.

Our everyday world is forever charged with titillating bits of information that keep our appreciation of the universe vital. Beyond mere attraction, when we look into the basic nature of attention itself, we have to wonder, "Does it possess us, or do we possess it? Does this force have a beginning, middle or end, a past, a future, a history and a fate? Or is attention simply present experience, which is the essence of 'being alive'?" Such questions invite us further into our own experience. The existential mysteries of attention lure us onto the path of spirituality with promises of a deeper appreciation of our lives.

We swim in a soup of minuscule details in which the grit of daily life may be as critical to our enlightenment as microscopic plankton is to a whale. People's hair colors, voice tones or the textures of the fabrics of their sweaters are all details that commonly slip beneath the radar of conscious attention. Yet, each subliminal feature affects our existence. Simply by paying attention, we stay involved in the world. The more attentive we are, the more we affect and are affected by the finer points of life. When awareness is cultivated and our receptivity is honed, every perception is a two-way communication. We radiate and we receive. A simple glance can impact another's life; likewise, when someone pays attention to us, they leave their stamp imprinted on that moment. Even if we wanted to avoid all contact with others we would still have to swim in the soup of interbeing. None of the molecules we breathe in and out are ours alone. Quite possibly the sufferings that fuel our compassion are but a few electrons shy of joy.

When our attention is allowed to wander aimlessly, it gives us a vague, illusory sense of freedom. Perhaps our bodies are lying on our beds but our minds are in another city and another time and the two seem divorced from each other. Yet, if we try to look at bewilderment as if it was a thing in itself, it vanishes. In fact, whenever we try to focus our attention on the past, it vanishes. The same is true of the future. Even when we are fully attentive of things happening in real time, we are left with nothing but pure presence.

In meditation, we endlessly peel the onions of our minds only to see layer after layer fall away. The conflicting emotions and neurotic beliefs about reality that have avoided scrutiny start to whither and die under the microscope of clear, present, focused and unbiased attention. As this self-examination gathers heat, everything evaporates into emptiness. The past and future dissolve into smoke, the present is purified and we are drawn into the flame of immediacy. In the end, the pristine glow of undefiled attention leaves no footprint other than its own inherent nobility.

3. Speed

We never see pictures or statues of the Buddha, Christ or Mohammed that depict speed or restlessness in any form. Rather, what has inspired people for centuries is their complete lack of franticness.

Imagine waking up from a nap feeling oddly disoriented. At first you seem a little dizzy but soon realize it is more than that. Apparently, while asleep, an unusual shift occurred in your mind. It is as if you are thinking in a foreign language, one that you don't speak and can't understand. While you were dozing, some unknown phenomenon rendered your private dialogue with yourself incomprehensible. With your inner voice speaking gibberish, all casual discursiveness makes you feel crazier. Reassured that there is still some semblance of awareness remaining, you stop trying to talk to yourself and just let your mind rest. Somehow you sense that, if you can simply be still and remain present, all will be fine.

I suspect most people view egolessness as a harrowing prospect. While we all seek happiness and yearn for calm amidst the storm, the specter of losing the companionship of our busy inner dialogue is terrifying, if not absurd. Consequently, we allow all kinds of unnecessary physical, mental and emotional dramas to fill our time and dominate our lives. Seemingly innocent preoccupations that entered our minds as guests have become full-time residents. We have since become so accustomed to their unending chorus of petty concerns that we have lost any reference point for silence. We have become like smokers proclaiming our intentions to quit but unable to stop ourselves from buying that last pack.

Naïve meditators often express concern that surrendering to nowness will kill their creative impulses or stunt their intellectual capacities. Actually, losing such abilities is probably the last thing we have to worry about. Enlightened people think beautifully and clearly and are incredibly creative. It seems that when discursive layers are stripped away, life becomes more vivid. Thinking doesn't stop, but it stops being a compulsive and desperate attempt to fill space.

When we sit, we discover how strong our addiction to speed actually is. More often than not, the forces of addiction are fiercer than we assumed. As soon as we hit the cushion we are bathed in an unending cascade of opinions about every subject known to mankind. We have attitudes about the weather, a new philosophy around food, endless comments about our rivals and a lifetime supply of fantasies. If we try to simply label our thoughts "thinking" and return to the breath, we find only a moment's relief before being quickly overcome with another wave of mental activity.

In daily life, speed takes on an even more insidious form: a mysterious sense of underlying urgency that fills our days with deadlines. Our self-imposed imperatives imply that if we fail to meet the urgent demands of a situation, we're toast. Meanwhile, we thrive on instant gratification, express lanes, fast food, car chases, rapid transit, high-speed internet and quick turnaround. We like things fast and we like them loud. It is no surprise that, every year, already high baseline levels of anxiety keep rising.

Like any addict approaching recovery, we have to begin by acknowledging that speed has power over us. On the warriorship path, pretense and denial simply don't work. It is possible to accept our mistakes without becoming bogged down in guilt or shame. Say we're cruising along a beautiful coastal highway and zip past a police car parked at a roadside tavern. A glance at the dashboard confirms that we have been going well over the speed limit, so immediately we start rehearsing excuses in anticipation of being pulled over. But, actually we don't have any valid excuses; there is no emergency and nothing worth risking our lives over. We simply spaced out and, without thinking, let speed take us over. Whether or not we are issued a ticket, even seeing the police car reminds us to slow down, to wake up and pry ourselves out of oblivion.

Relating to speed skillfully takes patience. Having awakened to the fact that we have been speeding, knee-jerk reactivity is just a continuation of our neurotic impulses. We need to do more than adjust our velocity. We need to regain our relationship with presence and move from undue urgency to grace and mindfulness. When we can no longer negotiate the curves effectively, accidents happen. Likewise, when our ability to return to Square One is compromised, our judgment is impaired. Speed fills the world with obstacles and unrelenting crises but we don't need to keep stubbornly pushing our agenda just to see how far and how fast we can go. Addicts are known for poor judgment. Drunks convince themselves that they can drive safely, only to take corners at sixty miles per hour. When our mental speed crosses the line, we need to accept those messages from the phenomenal world that suggest we slow down.

We don't need neurologists to tell us that acute fear and other tightly wound emotions stimulate more neurotransmitter activity than calm mental states. Obviously, compared to the intensified emotions that come with perilous situations, ordinary life is bland and boring. We are not Formula One drivers and we don't need to push ourselves closer and closer to the edge, just to feel more alive. Rather we need to come to terms with boredom. If we consistently up the ante, one day we will be unable to apply the brakes.

The setting sun mind roils in the world of the adrenalin rush and heightened arousal. Action films considered thrillers in the 1960s, 70s, 80s and even the 90s seem pretty lame today. Each new crop of movies and computer games compete to provide more sex, more crudity, an extra helping of violence. All this leads to deeper levels of depravity. The momentum behind these setting sun forces feeds on the acceleration of speed at the expense of decency and, while public standards sink lower with every passing season, we simply shrug.

Even a little speed diminishes our capacity to be kind. When we are at peace, we can afford to pay attention to others, but as we travel at higher speeds, more and more of our attention has to be focused on survival. Eventually, we withdraw our trust, our friends become opponents and simple human interactions are turned on their heads. Speed leaves us vulnerable to the common lust that Trungpa Rinpoche called 'P.O.O.' or *Power Over Others.* In today's world, we subtly compete for P.O.O. through money, social position or psycho-spiritual territoriality. As a result, the temporary thrill of defeating others trumps the satisfaction of developing genuine human connections. If allowed to go unchecked, this tendency can produce the animalistic, out-of-control, kill-or-be-killed aggression of the desperate junkie vying for a fix.

The buzz of winning and the agony of defeat are central to the addictive mentality. Drug use, crime, gambling, sexual promiscuity and violence all share the same needle. So when these exaggerated highs and lows are found in our 'normal' mood swings, we need to be careful. Our unwillingness to stay present can open deep chasms in our fragmentary affiliation with reality, which can then translate into deep wounds in our relationships.

We never see pictures or statues of the Buddha, Christ or Mohammed that depict speed or restlessness in any form. Rather, what has inspired people for centuries is their complete lack of franticness. In the forests, the deserts and the oceans, things happen precisely on schedule. A tree that has stood proudly for a hundred and fifty years will fall at exactly the right moment. Raindrops are never late to the pond. Taking a moment to step outside of speed allows our bodies and minds to settle back into synchronicity with each other and with nature. We find that pure love only happens in the present moment. The Buddha in the corner of the garden reminds us that nature herself is not driven by fanaticism.

4. Ordinariness

To regard the spiritual path as a holiday from daily life would be naïve.

For the next twenty seconds, please just stop reading and focus your attention on your breath. Simply pay attention to whatever sensations or sounds you connect with breathing. Let everything else simply arise and dissolve without judgment. In twenty seconds, I usually take three to four good breaths.

You may already do this from time to time. Intuitively, we know that practicing short mindfulness exercises throughout the day promotes good mental and spiritual hygiene. Regardless of whether we have been meditating for two weeks or twenty years, this type of practice is refreshing. Mindfulness brings attention home to the present moment. One moment mind is foggy, confused and diffused; the next it is clear and focused. If we can easily achieve such a result, why not make such an effort?

In Vermont, the fields and gardens come to life in the spring. After a long winter, as the snow melts and the sun breaks through the clouds, everything in the atmosphere seems vividly alive. Likewise, when nowness infiltrates our attention after we've been lost in daydreams, our whole being perks up. Fleeting and occasional flashes of clarity happen as a natural aspect of being alive. We can simply tolerate their haphazardness, or we can exploit these spontaneous moments of awareness by practicing intentional wakefulness. Little twenty to thirty second spurts of alertness sprinkled throughout the day can have a rewarding effect. Like adjusting the light in a room, coming back to nowness opens up our senses and brightens our hearts. We can't reach up into the sky and adjust the clouds, but tuning in to the immediacy of the breath makes us feel as if we have some control over our world.

Mindfulness refers to our capacity for placing awareness purposefully on an object and letting it rest there. We practice because despite our best intentions, distractions lay in wait, ready to ambush our focus. This is everyone's dilemma. Even after years of training, practitioners still get lost in the shadows of random thought. This struggle for stability and control has been dubbed the "Battle of Ego" and as with any conflict, the effort to stay on track consumes our inner resources. With time, the feeling of exhaustion becomes a cue to stop, take a few mindful breaths, and repair our broken connection with nowness.

By coming back to the present moment more often and staying longer, we start taming the untamed mind. Beneath the surface of our fascinations, our attention is a well-spring of pure awareness. Speed does not always have to be part of the equation. By intentionally relaxing our struggle and slowing down, an underlying silence starts to penetrate our experience.

So, let's try again. This time take at least thirty seconds to connect with the breath in the same way as before. Mindfully breathing in and out, take note of the rush of thoughts vying for your attention, but stay with it, not letting them distract you. The idea here is to remain focused. If it helps, any diversion can be silently labeled as "thinking "and then let go. After thirty full seconds or seven full breaths, in and out, see what happens.

I find it amazing that so much nagging self-talk can arise in the midst of this simple process. Invariably, some idea seems so important that it just can't wait. Yet, resting awareness on the breath has an illuminating and pacifying effect. Usually, people associate the notion of relaxation with letting one's hair down or taking a vacation, but here we are taking an anti-vacation. It's almost counter-intuitive. Rather than unwinding by taking a cruise down memory lane or drifting off on a flight of fancy, we find refreshment arises through restraint.

The idea of lying in the sand, sipping tequila, reading a novel and watching beautiful people in swimsuits sounds great, I know. But even on the most heavenly tropical beach, the mind still becomes restless. Why, because we see happiness as a future ideal, as something other than an appreciation of things as they are. Mundane happiness is usually based on the relief of boredom or some other irritating condition. When we are too hot, happiness is a swim in the pool. But after swimming for awhile, happiness is lying back down on our beach towel and ordering a drink. Of course, before long we start feeling hot again, and so on, and so on. This unending pursuit of gratuitous stimulation stops being fun after a few lifetimes. In the warrior's world, rather than fixating on the joy of scratching an itch, we see happiness as the joy of never having an itch to begin with.

When we confuse contentment with stimulation, and mistake grasping at entertainment for a real appreciation of life, we have fallen under the spell of the setting sun. To regard the spiritual path as a holiday from daily life would be naive. Meditation does not exempt us from doing the dishes or paying our bills. In fact, we can't simply reject the rest of our lives any more than we can reject the face we see in the mirror. In that sense, meditation can feel more like attending boot camp than luxuriating at a health spa. We might prefer to be soaking in a hot tub overlooking some tropical beach, but the inconvenient truth is that we have to acknowledge our ordinary neurotic and confused emotions. We can't afford to let sense pleasures sidetrack us from our quest for authenticity.

An authentic warrior does not seek relief by cutting corners or taking breaks from nowness. Warriors accept the twists and turns of fate as the natural landscape of the phenomenal world and feel at home wherever they are. Just as skiers and sailors relax by leaning into the fluidity of their sports, warriors rejuvenate themselves by embracing immediacy.

Let's return to the meditation cushion for one more simple exercise. This time, before we begin, take a reading of your own restlessness and anxiety on a subjective scale of one to ten. Whether you're at a six, a three or an eight doesn't matter; simply enjoy ten good inhalations and exhalations while staying present with the breath. Remember, the idea is to stay seated in stillness even when the pull of thinking is strong! Don't recoil from uncertainty, just let emotions roll over you. As you complete the tenth breath, take a new reading of your anxiety and restlessness. Has there been any shift? Regardless of the degree of change, simply taking notice has an effect. This is meditation.

5. Accepting Responsibility

This way of restraining discursive thinking and renewing presence is the core practice of warriorship. Such moment-to-moment spirituality attacks the roots of suffering like a guerilla army. It takes the battle to the back alleys, bus stops and marketplaces of our lives.

We are all familiar with the vivid spectrum of pain and pleasure known as the human realm. As human beings, we are infamous for clinging to the idea that happiness is just around the next corner. We torment ourselves with worries and grasp on to dreams that spawn disappointments again and again. Even when we succeed in carving out little islands of well being, they exist only within a larger sea of discontent. Generally, we stumble about in a blinding fog of discursive thought until we come face to face with the Buddha's First Noble Truth: that suffering permeates existence. We want what we don't have, have what we don't want and even when we have what we want, we suffer from the burden of maintaining it. Sooner than later, fresh and sweet turn to sour and bitter, and hope and fear seem to run the store.

It is hard to admit that we are out of step with reality. Yet all of our struggles and disappointments can be traced back to our unwillingness to accept the way things are. What cloud the picture, according to the Buddha, are our desires and attachments. Misery is only heightened when we rail against the present moment and attach ourselves to visions of the future or the past. So not only are we discontent, but according to the Second Noble Truth, the harder we cling to our ideas, fantasies and projections and reject our present experience, the more painful our lives become.

As we grow increasingly frustrated with our inaccurate and incomplete maps of reality, our suffering boils. Finally, when we have had enough pain and are ready to wake up, we start to observe the primordial laws of cause and effect or *karma*. We might think of ourselves as dogs on a leash and karma as our master, feeling twinges of pain and pleasure as life chafes against our collars. Sometimes, we find the flow and instinctively follow it; other times, we feel baffled and stuck, as if something is pulling us back. We seem condemned to learn by trial and error, and our mistakes are instructive. Yet, as we struggle, we keep falling into the traps we set for ourselves long ago.

Karma is not, as some might suggest, a matter of pre-determined fate: rather, it is a continuous and dynamic process. We may start the day relatively calm, feeling we haven't a care in the world, yet by the afternoon we are squirming like centipedes. "What happened?" we ask ourselves. How can things go from pleasure to pain without our seemingly doing anything? How can suffering arise out of thin air?

Being human, we are inquisitive by nature. We have to assume that things happen for a reason and that we have a role in how our lives play out. The people, places, things and events that we assume to be the causes of our pain, themselves have causes and conditions. And those causes and conditions have their own underpinnings, and so on without beginning. A destructive gulf-coast hurricane doesn't just pop out of nowhere on a beautiful sunny day. It is the result of a whole sequence of events involving the interplay of hot, dry sunny afternoons in the Sahara desert and the warming waters of the North Atlantic off the coast of Morocco. So many factors affect each moment in nature and each moment in our lives that it makes a full understanding of the details of cause and effect virtually impossible. However, we see the underlying principle and this gives us insight into the ways our mental habits and actions affect the world.

Everyone wants happiness and nobody wants misery, yet through our karmic clumsiness and raw ignorance, we reinforce pain. We eagerly plant carrot seeds, only to start praying desperately for cucumbers. Once our karmic seeds are sown, however, they are bound to sprout. Actions have definite results. If we plant carrots, we get carrots. If we plant the seeds of anger, we live in a world of anger. Crying out in protest, praying to gods and blaming others only make matters worse. Realizing that such responses have little efficacy, the Buddha taught that an accurate appreciation of karma is the basis of right action.

Karma does not imply original sin. But it does suggest that if we live our lives in a short-sighted manner, we are doomed to anguish. If our view of life is based on unconscious assumptions and beliefs, without concern for how our actions affect those around us, we are bound to suffer. Our negative moods become symptoms of disconnectedness. When things go well we feel powerful and good, but with the first hint of negative feedback, out comes the blame card. One minute we are arrogant and proud, the next minute we are casting ourselves as victims. The pain of *victimitis* reveals the weaknesses in the humpty-dumpty strategy of self-righteousness. Even the most eloquent sermons proclaiming the highest moral superiority cannot put a fractured past back together again.

Being enlightened, the Buddha clearly saw how the unconscious mind functions. In the Third Noble Truth, he was able to articulate the most fundamental principle of karma: when ignorant assumptions about reality are set aside, our nightmares come to an end. Consequently, the way out of our karmic torment is through awakening to our cravings and ceasing to generate them.

What the Buddha offered as the principle means to accomplish this reversal was the practice of mindfulness. On the meditation cushion, we accomplish insight not by entering into deep philosophical debates with ourselves about the meaning of life but by noticing how our relationship with reality shifts when our thoughts tear us away from the present moment. As we gently guide our attention back to the breath, we appreciate the virtues of staying rooted in nowness. We find we can accept the way things are without imposing our opinions as ultimate truths. Gone is the need to solidify passion, aggression and ignorance and project our dissatisfaction onto everything and everyone.

Off the cushion, the same insight is applied to every other aspect of our lives. If we find ourselves storming about in a reactive mood or distracted by some frivolous project, rather than becoming angry, again and again we steer ourselves back to the present moment. This way of restraining discursive thinking and renewing presence is the core practice of warriorship. Such moment-to-moment spirituality attacks the roots of suffering like a guerilla army. It takes the battle to the back alleys, bus stops and marketplaces of our lives. Gradually, wisdom finds its way into our kitchens, bedrooms, offices and playgrounds, and the usefulness of mindfulness discipline becomes unquestionable.

In the fourth of his Four Noble Truths, known as the Eightfold Path, the Buddha taught how to apply mindfulness to every aspect of our existence. As we bring this truth into clearer focus, we can plumb the depths of our being and observe all the habitual patterns that arise, appreciate their insidious effects and apply an antidote. We might be discouraged by all the impurities that become apparent but rather than arousing shame, guilt and blame, we can see dirt in the rinse water as a sign that something is coming clean. The painful discovery of self-deception can be good news. However, instead of rushing to repair a fractured ego, we allow time for humbleness and inquisitiveness. Actually, we start to appreciate the cracks because they allow rays of truth to filter through.

In the clearer light of awareness, we discover that things are not all bad. We discover that the basic ground of our being is fundamentally good and that it has been from the very beginning. Grasping this gives us encouragement to wake up. The mega-message of the Four Noble Truths and all of the teachings on karma is that whatever occurs in the mind is ultimately workable. With a more wakeful understanding of cause and effect, we can make wiser and more compassionate choices. When this appreciation dawns, we realize that even the best of scapegoats will never cause us as much suffering as we have caused ourselves.

6. Raising the Gaze

Relaxing into the present moment connects us to our intrinsic sanity, while raising our gaze in the spirit of vipashyana means opening our hearts and looking the world in the eye.

In our meditation practice, two basic modes of exploration work together to create momentum on the path, *relaxing into the present moment* and *raising the gaze*. Buddhists often refer to these two practices by their Sanskrit names- **shamatha** and **vipshyana**- the development of peace and the cultivation of panoramic awareness.

Relaxing into the present moment occurs as a result of mindfulness. The shamatha practice of calmly abiding relies on a simple technique of focusing attention on one object without straying into fragmented, discursive thoughts. Although it sounds easy, this practice often presents a challenge that beginning meditators find daunting. "Is it really possible to rest the mind on something as boring as breathing without constant distraction?" they ask. The answer is yes, but to do so takes time, practice and perseverance. Eventually, stability increases and longer periods of sustained presence develop and from the murky depths of haziness and confusion, the radiant lotus of clear awareness emerges.

The peace that arises from shamatha is compared to a calm lake in which the precise perceptions of vipashyana naturally arise. As the surface of the lake settles, the bigger picture comes into focus. An inquisitive, open mind can hold a clear reflection of the sky and distant hillsides. It can also see into its own depths. So, the practice of raising one's gaze is both a figurative and literal experience. A photographer is likely to notice more colors or see ordinary objects differently with a camera in her hands. Likewise, the practitioner of vipashyana sees things with new eyes. Aspects of truth that have been obscure suddenly seem obvious. Clear seeing requires that attention be somewhat stable, but once we have truly settled, fresh insights dawn on us with surprising regularity.

Relaxing into nowness has always fostered insight. Formal meditation simply moves that process along. Raising the gaze may produce delightful "Aha!" moments, but even these have to be abandoned lest the extra effort of trying to recreate them becomes distracting. Shamatha and vipashyana work in tandem like the risers and treads on a staircase. Each stair is built on the one below; once we have taken a step and assumed our balance, we keep climbing. When we fall asleep in the peace of calm abiding, we lose our enthusiasm for growing. Likewise, we can be swept away by speculation or fantasy if we raise our gaze prematurely.

When the yogi Siddhartha sat in meditation, he settled his mind just as we try to settle ours. The insights that dawned on him may have been as important to human evolution as the discovery of fire. But such wisdom was not unique to the young Buddha. Every generation of practitioners rediscovers the same truths, over and over again, and each awakened flash is just as illuminating to us as it was to him. True realization is always fresh because it can only occur in the present moment.

The warrior's mind is geared toward waking up; whereas the cowardly mind is always looking for the perfect conditions for zoning out. The faster things move and the louder the background noise, the faster we settle for superficiality. Like sleepy commuters peering through the grimy windows of a bullet train zooming through the bowels of a gray city at breakneck speed, our lives become a blur. Sadly, we forget about trying to wake up; all we care about is getting home and shutting down. As we cower and lower our gazes and plug our iPods into our ears or bury our heads in a novel, we go on autopilot. With the thermostat set at a constant 70 degrees, our lives become the ideal breeding ground for ignorance and inauthenticity.

Ironically, it is our need for tranquility that underlies the urge to put up walls and withdraw from the rat-race. But despite our efforts to find refuge from the madness, we seldom find silence. Particularly in man-made urban environments, true calm is increasingly rare. This is especially sad because the nurturing effect of stillness is so critical to human survival. One glance around the subway car reveals more fancy electronic devices attached to more people's ears than ever before. Unfortunately, such paraphernalia only add further weight to our already heavy psychic workloads. Rather than strengthening our mindfulness, turning up the music and pounding to the beat ultimately drains our subliminal stamina.

150,000 years ago, our ancestors reveled in their ability to create a spark and ignite a blaze from almost nothing. Today, very few people would be able to start a fire without matches or a lighter, even if their lives depended on it. This loss of connection to the raw goodness of nature has weakened us. Taking nature for granted has put us in peril and our faith in gadgetry has betrayed us. No generation has ever owned so much 'stuff' and at the same time been saddled with so many unfulfilled expectations. We have invested heavily in the dream of convenience; yet here we are, wading through the flotsam and jetsam of social disrepair.

At this juncture, we need the practices of shamatha and vipashyana to reconnect us to our intrinsic sanity. Raising our gaze means opening our hearts and looking the world in the eye. We have to do this. When we cower and shut down very little of what we see, hear, smell or touch actually penetrates our hearts, and without a heart connection we just go through the motions. It is time to look up and rediscover how to ignite the flames of insight. To survive, we have to learn this simple act. And if we do, perhaps within a few short generations every human being will be able to harness their inherent enlightenment.

I remember being on vacation in the Yucatan with my father many years ago. One mildly overcast morning, we decided to go snorkeling and found our way to a small cove and an almost vacant resort. Ambling down to the shoreline, we came upon an older couple from Chicago, occupying a terrace built above a sea wall. The man was firmly ensconced in a beach chair, drinking coffee and attempting to read a magazine. His wife, seated across from him, wore a light blouse over a bathing suit and greeted us as we approached with our diving gear in hand. As we exchanged pleasantries, she shared that she had hoped to coax her husband into the water; however he was clearly not interested in swimming. Neither was she interested in his magazines. I felt like we had walked into a slightly comical standoff. He wanted to relax and read; she was irritated and sick of just sitting around the cabana. Of course, she would not dare to go swimming alone, and he needed her company. The interaction had the scent of an old, tired ritual.

Apart from this couple, we seemed to be alone. A light wind ruffled the coconut palms and the dull, silvery ocean was totally blasé in a tropical paradise kind of way. The morning haze promised to burn off soon, revealing a typically splendid morning sun. Having waded into the rolling waves, my father and I started paddling toward a sheltering reef about 100 feet from shore.

Within the next few moments everything changed. I left behind the familiar world of idle conversation, beach chairs and coffee and entered an amazing labyrinth of underwater coral reefs, none of which had been apparent from the shore. Before I could adjust my snorkel, my attention was swept up by a school of brilliant yellow and black shapes darting to my left. Meanwhile, to my right, flashes of silver and gold glittered in unison. Seconds later, with the precision of a military marching band, a thousand minnows gracefully swerved off at a sharp angle. Walls of flickering fins feinted to the right, then up, then down as if following an invisible conductor's baton. In less than a minute, I was thoroughly entranced.

Floating on the surface, I noticed a small set of eyes belonging to a vividly purple entity poking out from between two huge multicolored cauliflowers. To its right, an octopus fluttered while a sea snake lay curled up like a snarl of discarded rope in the hollows of a boulder. Out of the corner of my visor, a peacock turned out to be a fan shaped coral waving in the underwater breeze as two miniature sea horses, suspended like ornamental hummingbirds, ambled by. Beyond the next rock, an eel slithered into a crevasse and a family of crabs scrambled across the sandy floor. The scene just kept unraveling as my mind swarmed with sheer delight.

When my father finally signaled me toward the shore maybe an hour and a half later, it was hard to pull away. The pulsating undersea universe was far more enticing than lunch. Nonetheless, tramping out on to the beach, we again passed the old couple, under their umbrella in beach chairs. The sun was now quite hot and they had donned sunglasses, but other than that nothing much had changed.

"Hello" I said, with the excitement of the dive still in my eyes.

"Good morning!" the woman replied, putting down her Newsweek. "It seems you enjoyed your swim?"

"Enormously!" I replied. "Isn't the reef great?"

My father asked her husband if he enjoyed snorkeling. "Not really interested," said the man.

"Hal doesn't like to swim much." his wife blurted. "We come here every year! I think this is the fifth year now and I keep saying we should try it, but he won't. So neither of us has gone; but people do seem to enjoy it!"

Looking back at the reef, I realized that from the angle of the terrace it was impossible to see what lay beneath the undulating surface of the water. "You don't know what you're missing." I said.

7. Kindness

Wherever there is joy or pain, there is a basis for kindness; such is the fragile ecology that unites us all.

Nature has served us with an ultimatum. We can either wake up and find some way to resolve our differences or face eviction from this planet. The alternatives are few. Since this Earth is the only functioning life support system within trillions of miles, we have little choice but to work together. Torturing each other and languishing in selfishness are no longer options. Our only hope lies in developing greater compassion. As daunting as that may sound, the welfare of the entire living universe may depend on the kindness of the human heart.

Kindness is intrinsic to life in all of its myriad forms. Human beings require benevolence simply to be born. Deprived of the loving attention of caregivers, infants wither and die within hours of leaving their mothers' wombs. Yet, when babies are nurtured with love, the result is breathtaking. In nature, the role of kindness is poignant yet simple- compassion and genuine attention are life-supporting; neglect and invalidation are devastating. With the proper care, we flourish; without it, we flounder. And as it is with children, so it is with gardens, animals, nations and planets.

Even the most callous of brutes with the hardest armor of machismo is capable of generating at least a spark of kindness. If we could examine the hearts of Mao Tse Tung, Hitler, Pol Pot, Saddam Hussein or Stalin, we would probably find that they all harbored tender feelings in some form. Vicious beasts, mass murderers and bloodied terrorists all have soft spots for something or someone if we look closely enough. Those who cannot shed a tear for their dying grandmothers, their children, lovers, pet pythons or themselves, can at least moisten their eyes for their fantasies.

The amazing human heart is a masterpiece of emotional engineering. Somewhere inside each of us, small flames of kindness burn like pilot lights, ready to ignite us with love. If we have sad or moving reactions, the gas gets turned up and the flames of passion surge. When compassion wanes, our heart-flames flirt with extinction. Regardless of whom we think we are or where we live, a kind of Morse code sustains our existence and allows us to communicate in a language beyond words. As our hearts beat out the dots and dashes of hello and goodbye, we share a kind of nonlinear, emotional poetry with embedded messages that define our nature.

Even a lifetime of a hundred years can be broken down into individual heartbeats. The basic building blocks of time- the seconds, minutes, hours and years that we have imposed on eternity, all stem from the simple thump of life, that universal pulse within our chests. That same simple rhythmic *paDump, paDump, paDump* that drives us forward into our days and fills our sleep with dreams at night is the source of all music. When we pry open the doors of empathy and listen with responsive ears, the drum of kindness reminds us who we are. When we hold a newborn and feel its soft skin against our cheeks, we feel its tender little heart beating with the joy of renewal. In the same way, when we feel the lack of a pulse in a corpse, we are tempered by the chill of mortality.

Wherever there is joy or pain, there is a basis for kindness; such is the fragile ecology that unites us all. Negative emotions do not sit well with the warrior spirit. A life deprived of the oxygen of kindness is a living hell. There is no satisfaction in kissing a mask, no sincerity in a painted smile and no joy in a life devoid of compassion. When we lose our faith in kindness we become vulnerable to every affliction that can turn a life sour. The cries of the abused and their abusers echo throughout our streets and our jails. Even the finest neighborhoods overflow with victims of untreated pain. Nowhere is there a space or time that cannot be improved by kindness.

Tibetan Buddhism teaches that the awakened heart or *bodhicitta* is absolutely essential to spiritual evolution. For the flower of wisdom to bloom, it needs to be rooted in an open heart. If we want our children to flourish, we need to train them to be generous and to think of others. Developing genuine instincts for kindness today will provide them the keys to future prosperity. Trungpa Rinpoche taught that the power to awaken superhuman qualities is within each of us. He was not suggesting that we transform into Superman, Wonder Woman or the Incredible Hulk. Rather, he was implying that we could become the incredibly kind Joe Schmidt or the delightfully compassionate Jane Doe. True benevolence should always be part of our decision making processes. If it is, we can inspire not only those we love, but everyone.

Our existence and everything it represents will soon disperse into the universe. Our houses will disappear, our names will be forgotten and our memories will evaporate, yet acts of kindness reverberate through time. There is no need to wait until the last minute to make kindness our final signature. Every time we exit a room, we leave a legacy. If we leave behind a life marked by simple acts of kindness, our children and all future generations of beings will inherit a cleaner, more uplifted world.

8. The Dance of Fear

When we accept the invitation to dance with fear,
every encounter is regarded as a steppingstone to
fearlessness.

To be a warrior means to live life without pretense. In simple terms, this means becoming intimate with ourselves in a way that leaves no room for self-deception. The warrior's character is refined by constantly dancing with fear. Every day challenges the warrior to go deeper, to uncover, to acknowledge and to accept things that might otherwise be ignored. This dance of intimacy leads to the undoing of habitual patterns. It invites the warrior to step out of the shadows of cowardice, shed the shoddy armor of arrogance and venture into the humbleness of what Suzuki Roshi called 'Beginner's Mind'.

If we are interested in becoming authentic warriors, we must regard our dance with fear as serious business. Just as we would never regard a samurai sword as a toy, meditation should not be regarded as a hobby or a self-improvement project. Dedicating one's life to wakefulness is quite different than taking an exercise class to lose weight. It is a powerful and precise tool with the capacity to cut through the root of suffering and expose the truth of what is. As Shambhala warriors, how we employ this sharp instrument defines our lives.

Dancing with fear puts us on the spot, not on the defensive. In her often quoted essay, *Our Deepest Fear,* Marianne Williamson writes, *"Our deepest fear is not that we are inadequate. Our deepest fear is that we are powerful beyond measure."* If we look into the mirror of meditation with that attitude, can we see our fragilities and our strengths, not as enemies but as partners? If so, the challenge of fear takes on a different hue. When we are no longer afraid of our strengths or our weaknesses, our brilliance or our shadows, fearlessness becomes a genuine expression of who we really are.

Once, while giving a talk to a group of about thirty people, I asked the audience to list words and phrases that express aspects of fear. At first, people offered a few obvious synonyms: nervous, terrified, scared, afraid and so on. After that came hesitation, ambivalence, dread, paranoia, worry and panic. As we explored further, a fascinating mural began to emerge. Voices piped in with words like coyness, apprehension, wishy-washiness, insecurity, anxiety, aloofness and concern, trepidation, fright, mistrust, shyness, angst, hyper vigilance, caution, foreboding, uneasiness, timidity, reluctance, and guardedness. And we were just getting started.

Perhaps our language contains so many expressions for fear because when we sense peril, it affects us in such a variety of ways. It would be a gross oversimplification to say that when our brains release adrenalin we are driven to fight or flee. In moments of intense anxiety we may freeze, vomit, scream, laugh manically or dissociate, depending on a whole host of factors. Yet no matter what reactive mechanism we employ, if we find the presence to stay with the fear and simply acknowledge the felt sense of our body in that moment, the force of our reaction loses its momentum. When we are able to be truly inquisitive in the midst of a rushing torrent of fear, without judging or blaming or taking allegiance with any form of solidification, we find ourselves softening and opening, and the intensity slowly unravels.

Often scars from the past affect our ability to love and be loved in the present moment. We know that the social genes of apprehension and distrust can pass from one generation to the next as easily as they pass between villages. Similarly, we see how a traumatic event can inflict or re-open a painful wound and shudder as the rancid pus of repressed anger oozes out. Maybe twenty years ago our wife or husband walked into the kitchen and announced, "I no longer love you, I want a divorce!" or an officious voice on the other end of a telephone stated, "I regret to inform you that your friend has been killed." At the time, we winced with pain or were overcome with shock. Maybe our shoulder muscles tightened into a knot, our lungs struggled to fill with air or a line formed on our brow.

Now, twenty years later, we have grown accustomed to pain in our upper back and permanent wrinkles. Storm after storm and wave after wave of energized thoughts have rolled over those tense shoulders driving reactive emotional grooves deeper into our necks, chests, groins and stomachs. At some unconscious level, the world is still a mine field, riddled with all kinds of triggers. Each time a memory of a traumatic event bubbles up in our subconscious, another anxious flood of toxic neurotransmitters is sent cascading through our synapses. Our nervous systems still send out messages of alarm to the heart, lungs, colon and our aged muscles still remain on alert like tired sentries.

It's no wonder we develop so many aches, pains and illnesses as we age. We have been bracing ourselves against fear's tyranny for decades. Past traumas and projected future threats have undermined us and ransacked our reserves for so many years that we are left eroded and worn down like cracks in an old sea wall. Long after the initial flood has receded, little tidal pools of tension still linger in the form of headaches, muscle aches and fatigue. We have been cringing so long that we have literally forgotten how to relax. Rather than dancing with fear we have been running from it or, at the very least, hiding.

Meditation teaches us not to assign blame, but rather to reassign our awareness. Although the energy of fear seems to come from the past or future, it actually happens within the present moment. Mindfulness allows us to meet the sparkling fresh quality of fear with unadulterated clarity, and to let it go.

When we accept the invitation to dance with fear, every encounter is regarded as a steppingstone to fearlessness. If terror arises in our throats, we look into it. If it moves from our neck to our jaw, we follow it. If it tries to take up residence in our shoulders or in our guts, we breathe our awareness into it and massage it with a kind of cautious curiosity. We develop the confidence and skill of a good dance partner, so we can feel fear pass though us like a wave. Without over-reacting, we tune into the pulse of fear, its fluidity and its aliveness, and as this process evolves, everything changes.

Presence disarms the trigger points of anxiety, diffuses the charges of paranoia and allows us to remain composed. As we sweep up the last pockets of resistance and ferret out the remnants of fear, we don't need to resort to further aggression or re-fortify our defenses. Instead of whole new rounds of tyranny we can foster compassion for our own struggle. Our fearlessness brings peace and strength to both mind and body so we can look fear straight in the eye and smile. Rather than hiding in the shadows, we can accept fear's invitation to step forward and fully inhabit our dignity.

9. Hesitation

As long as we believe that we are fundamentally flawed,
we will continually fall prey to hesitancy.

Sitting practice, when truly taken to heart, calls into question our core beliefs and assumptions about how things are. Establishing a daily meditation routine can really throw a monkey wrench into a life-style based on habitual patterns with a firm allegiance to the status quo. It places new demands on our time and our psyches, demands that we may be hesitant to meet with complete conviction. Yet, we step beyond hesitation every time we take the posture of a warrior. Sitting with a strong back and an open front, prepared to accept the present moment as it is, is an act of courage. We learn to hold our seats, and remain realistic and flexible. Like skilled sailors using both wind and current to guide a ship into harbor, we learn to harness and work positively with whatever arises in our minds. Certainly, challenging our doubts takes courage, skill and practice, and it is reasonable to expect that we will be swept away by hopes and fears, again and again. In this way, seasoned warriors, like salty old seafarers, eventually come to trust in the basic workability of life.

Ego, in the guise of cowardice, is always ready to highlight our weaknesses and sabotage our efforts. When we squirm in our seats, slump with discouragement and let our minds be blown off course, the whole thing seems like a colossal struggle. Without a firm trust in basic goodness, we can easily freeze in fear or be mired in ambivalence. We become so busy turning away from the onslaught of reality that we can't move forward. As long as we believe that we are fundamentally flawed, we will continually fall prey to hesitancy.

Confidence in our true nature opens up the path to fearlessness, whereas ambivalence is a subtle trap that sets us back, even when we think we are moving forward. If we hum and haw with indecision, shifting weight from one foot to the other with the relentless rhythm of uncertainty, we remain stuck in neutral. We may wear holes in our socks or develop painful blisters on our feet, but we get nowhere. Unless we shift into gear, how can we expect to progress along the path?

We simply cannot afford to be fooled by the layers of doubt and hesitation that fog our minds. I grew up in the Pacific Northwest, a place where it can be cloudy for months on end. As a depressed teenager, occasionally I would forget that the sky was blue. Grey rainclouds filled the sky, day after day, until life became chronically dreary. Of course, just when I thought that I would never see a clear sky again, the sun would poke through. That period of my life left me with an appreciation of how dark and enduring the clouds of despair can be. Conversely, I came to realize how just precious one hour of sunshine can be and what immeasurable relief and joy a clear blue sky can bring.

When we lack faith in the boundless nature of our minds, we tend to follow the meditation technique reluctantly and haphazardly. When meditation is persistently soggy, it is easy to identify with our history of failure. Our shiftless meanderings take on a sense of solidity and we forget about the sky of basic goodness. Although we make great plans to meditate, we end up playing computer games or watching television. In a frenzy of optimism, we might commit to a bold set of New Year's resolutions. However, by the second week of January, the cloudbanks of hesitation start rolling in. As our resolve weakens and our inspiration fades, the cycle of depression is renewed.

This type of hesitation is like the insecurity of a novice swimmer. Before we learn to swim, we fear sinking or drowning and doubt our capacity to stay afloat. We desperately cling to floating objects or to the side of the pool, obsessed with safety. Meditators who are afraid to let go of egoic reference points, reinvent and pervert the meditation technique and end up clinging to thoughts and emotions like bits of flotsam or driftwood littering the waters of the mind. Instead of labeling thoughts and coming back to the breath, they label the breath and go back to thoughts. Threatened by visions of non-existence, they take refuge in the confused emotions rather than relaxing into the buoyancy of the present moment. This aversion to trusting space is what Trungpa Rinpoche used to refer to as ego's unwillingness to attend its own funeral.

However, since we have made it this far, and even donned our bathing suits, sitting on the edge of the pool and refusing to swim feels awkward. Intuitively, we know that if we are to progress along the path, some kind of leap is necessary. We need to shift our perspective from regarding nowness as the unsettling and intimidating instability of events to joyfully embracing immediacy as a source of refreshment and renewal. Once we learn to swim, our approach to water changes forever. In much the same way, as we gain confidence in basic goodness, each moment of meditation reinvigorates our sense of presence. Moving from cowardice to bravery, we approach impermanence and uncertainty from a different angle.

In the middle of our practice, a gap forms in the clouds of thought. Feeling the warmth of the Great Eastern Sun, we may be inspired to relax; however, as hesitation drifts back in, we lose our nerve and a whole new train of commentary begins. "If I let go completely, will I still be able to hold a job?" Such hesitations are, as Eckhart Tolle points out, just ego's subtle strategies to avoid presence.

When we finally tire of lazily tapping our feet in hesitation, we dive in and fully inhabit our lives. Each leap into nowness gives us another taste of freedom. We start to realize that our ability to be present is not contingent on going to school, accumulating fancy credentials or paying 'dues' for years and years. The Tibetans have a saying that sometimes an ordinary corpse is found in the bed of a great scholar. So, while learning is certainly not a bad thing, if we use study as an excuse for putting off our practice, our knowledge will be weak. Meanwhile, whatever calls us back to Square One is valid. When the truth hits us, we simply don't have the luxury of endless philosophizing or procrastination. The smell of burning toast or the sound of a siren might jolt us back into the present moment as effectively as any book. After all, that ambulance we hear in the distance could be coming for us!

It is not about how we get back to the here and now; it's about what we do once we arrive. Warriorship is a commitment to staying awake. When we return to presence, not as a lofty concept, but as direct experience, things become vividly clear and alive. Our challenge is to simply enter into this moment, as it is, without trying to alter it in any way. Cutting through hesitation means taking the posture of 'no more excuses'.

I once shared a telephone conversation with Trungpa Rinpoche at a time when my life seemed to be falling apart at an alarming rate. On that particular day, I was drowning in a rushing torrent of thoughts and flailing about in self-pity. Auspiciously, I had the opportunity to speak to Rinpoche about some other business. It must have been perfectly evident to him that I was going through hell, so, hoping for a little sympathy, I started to share my story. At first he seemed to listen patiently, however, after a minute or more of my moaning, he asked me, "What did you eat for breakfast?"

"Breakfast? You mean this morning, today? What did I eat for breakfast this morning?" I stammered, somewhat nonplussed. "Um, cereal and toast, I guess! Yeah, I think I had Raisin Bran and toast!"

"That's good." he replied. Then there was a long pause that caught me off guard. After a moment he added quite pointedly, "Don't think too much! Keep it simple!"

Suddenly, all my problems seemed workable and I relaxed. To this day, I reflect on that conversation. "Keeping it simple!" has been yet another of those quintessential instructions for my life.

When we are stuck in hesitation, we need to leap out of stale ambivalence into the freshness of no reference point. This may mean letting go of the sides of the pool and getting wet. Without thinking too much, we will soon start kicking our feet to stay afloat.

In the midst of our reverie, we might perk up our ears. Lo and behold, suddenly the world is full of sounds: from airplanes in the distant sky, to a ticking clock, to the roar of the brook. We might slow down and taste our food or pause long enough to feel our breath crossing the threshold of our nostrils. Too much thinking clogs our perceptual arteries. We need to suspend our struggle with the way things are and relax into the naturalness of this moment. By surrendering in this way, we come to trust our buoyancy. As Sakyong Mipham Rinpoche says, our minds become our allies, rather than our adversaries.

And remarkably, when we let go, the rest of the world relaxes as well. We don't need to make a big splash. One moment we are dry and the next, we are wet, and before we have time to think, we are swimming.

10. The Wisdom of Emotions

Forming an allegiance with the basic goodness of others depends on our first making friends with ourselves.

Sitting meditation is not about bracing ourselves against the cold north wind of confusion and irritability. When we take a good posture, we do not just become stoic little statues of the Buddha. Rather, as warriors, we embody an attitude of fearlessness, gentleness and inquisitiveness. Since, at times, the wind of the mind can be very strong, expecting to survive its ferocity each time we confront it would be naive. Our challenge is to learn to take advantage of the wind and work with it, again much like when sailing a boat. This is the essence of our discipline. Certainly, confronting the onslaught of our emotions and doubts takes courage, and without skill and practice we can expect to be swept away, over and over. Yet, as our mindfulness matures, it becomes apparent that it is possible to ride the windiness of emotions. Not only do we become adept at harnessing their energies, but by taking a keen interest in each emotional moment, we marvel as the layers of passions and furies unravel to reveal unique aspects of wisdom.

How do we, as aspiring warriors, make the leap from "one of the worst so-and-so's in the world", into men and women of dignity? How do we stop our minds from racing out of control and find the means to express our humanity with grace and honor? From the moment that we step onto this path, we are gently encouraged to not run away from difficult situations or events, but instead to sit still amidst the turmoil until we have become intimate with ourselves. Since ego generates emotional responses to everything and everyone, learning to remain present in moments of intensity is the key to refining our essential decency.

When we are young and naive, we generally think that our actions don't matter. We believe that we can afford to act capriciously and plan to live forever, somehow immune from cause and effect. Our formative minds may feast on abstract ideas of freedom while our knee-jerk reactions display little in the way of genuine appreciation of how our behaviors affect others. Youth is notorious for idealism, rebelliousness and the vim and vigor of lustiness, but with the onslaught of dreaded maturity, we begin to see the wisdom of modesty and restraint.

Today's world is rife with displays of raw emotional crudity. We can turn on the television in the middle of the morning and watch jilted, jealous and intoxicated men and women verbally berating their former friends, lovers or suitors. We can indulge our voyeuristic appetites for unscripted physical violence from the cocoon-like comfort of our living rooms, while some poor, devastated victim is egged on by jeering mobs of bloodthirsty onlookers. The very fact that such programming is deemed suitable for a national audience is a sad statement of how the setting sun mentality is affecting our culture.

Of course, regardless of why we feel outrage, it is imperative to learn to trim the sails of our own minds before we set off to save the world. Any allegiance with the basic goodness of others depends on our first having made friends with ourselves. True compassion is not clogged by distorted storylines and neurotic emotional reactions. So, a warrior's approach to dealing with disturbing emotions can be seen as a three-fold process. First, emotions are acknowledged without cowering or apology. Secondly, having been acknowledged, emotional energy deserves respect. We can touch, taste and truly get to know the wind behind our mood and the intensity behind our voice. Finally, having demystified and fully felt the feeling, it is possible to remain present as we skillfully direct our energy or elegantly allow it to dissipate.

Acknowledging anger, fear, jealousy, guilt, shame or any emotion is not as easy as it sounds. Because of prior pain, we may be intimidated by strong feelings and want to ward them off or deny their power. For example, to be overtaken by sudden feelings of outrage can be intensely uncomfortable. So, immediately we may start looking for an exit. If denying such feelings doesn't work, we start blaming others. Both denial or blame suggest we are afraid of our fear, embarrassed about our embarrassment, or ashamed of our shame. Trungpa Rinpoche called this *"negative negativity"*. Under the spell of this common form of dysregulated reactivity, we berate ourselves for feeling or behaving badly. Rather than truly respecting our emotions, we come to 'hate ourselves'. Applying psychic pressure of this sort doesn't help; it just makes us feel worse. Eventually, the snowballing effect of negative negativity develops into an emotional numbness or a kind of neurotic fugue.

Retreating behind predictable reactions in the hope of shielding ourselves from intensity only confuses things. The reflexive impulse to turn away from emotional energy leads to insincerity and other forms of deceit. We may think we are hiding our wound or masking our pain behind cowardice, jealousy and anger, but our true feelings are usually obvious to others.

Those who work with difficult children, or emotionally-challenged adults for that matter, can appreciate the old saying that *'those who need love the most are usually the hardest to love'*. The same principle applies to those parts of ourselves that we chronically reject or deny. Behind our inner walls there may be whole psychic neighborhoods that we are afraid to enter. So, it is good to begin by acknowledging those passions or furies that freak us out the most. And, as we proceed, it is important to remember that we cower for a reason. Fear is not a crime, nor is it a virtue; it is a reaction. Everyone experiences fear because the world is dangerous. However, while we all long to feel safe, maintaining our integrity in the face of fear is the warrior's way.

This takes us to the second stage in this process: actually touching, tasting and getting to know our feelings on a more intimate level. The nitty gritty of freeing ourselves from the grasp of any emotion involves feeling its texture or listening to its story without becoming hooked by its tentacles. Respecting an emotion exposes the real nature of the emotion. In the spaciousness of meditation we can accept and study our emotions with an almost scientific yet kindly inquisitiveness. Touching the actual energy of an emotion might mean stopping in the middle of an argument and checking in with the tone of our voice or the heat of our passion. We might say to ourselves, "How interesting! I am feeling angry, right now! This is anger, and it is what it is. This is my chance to study it." When annoyed, or sad, or lustful or depressed we can seize the opportunity to feel what annoyance is like, what sadness is like, and so on, and even ask "Who is generating this energy?", "Who is the 'reactor'?"

When we touch an emotion with this kind of inquiry, the answer does not come in words, but rather in the unspoken language of nowness. It is like looking in the mirror and trying to see a memory. The immediacy of emotional energy transcends and overpowers the spiraling neurotic patterns that we associate with reason. Genuinely feeling the fleeting quality of any sentiment reveals the insubstantial nature of our supposedly solid personalities. Surges of intensity turn thoughts into dreamlike, transient, phantom energies that pass like storms moving through the sky. Letting ourselves feel their true textures has the effect of releasing us from their grasp. So, feeling the texture of our fear becomes the way out of fear. Rather than avoiding the present moment, we lean into it.

Somehow, it seems ironic that acknowledging, touching and tasting any emotion, no matter how strong or aversive it may be, actually loosens fixation. Yet, as the solidity of the emotion breaks down, the third step- letting go- happens effortlessly. When we can see that the nature of awareness is like a moving river, all feelings, from our most significant and justifiable grudges to spurious bouts of sentimentality, are clearly marked by impermanence. Waves of fury may come and go and surges of passion may arise and deflate, but everything is part of the same current. In the course of our sitting practice, we taste the effervescent quality of anger, disgust, frustration, or for that matter, happiness, again and again. At first, it is like tasting and savoring a slice of fresh pear, a bite of aged cheese or a piece of fine chocolate. But after the fifth serving, we notice that whatever we eat dissolves in our mouth and is gone. And so we move on.

11. Resistance

When there is nowhere else to go and nothing else to do, we finally surrender to things as they are.

I think I understand how a visitor from another galaxy might perceive the planet Earth as some kind of karmic penal colony. Given our neurotically predictable, antlike behaviors, they might easily assume that earthlings are under the control of some sinister force with an erratic will. Our strangely passionate, communal enthusiasm for wars, Superbowls, political rallies and mass religious gatherings might best be explained as the result of powerful hypnotic instincts embedded into our psyches by an omniscient force greater than ourselves.

The perennial question of free will remains one of the most pressing theological concerns of the 21st Century. There may always be those who believe in a predestined fate and others who feel that the universe unfolds quite randomly. Fundamentalists, who strictly believe in "God-the-Creator", face increasingly convincing challenges to their orthodoxy every day. Some are convinced that things have spun so far out of control that there is no turning back, others put their faith in divine intervention. Still others feel that theism is sadly misleading, no matter what form it takes, and that we simply cannot rely on forces outside ourselves to save the world.

To the theist world, Buddhism presents a confusing paradox. Here we have a tradition that does not ascribe to beliefs in external entities, be they gods or devils, yet, without postulating any solidity, recognizes that all present conditions have their precedents. Buddhists see the convoluted circumstances of our current lives as the results of past actions while acknowledging that the present moment offers an ongoing opportunity for transcendence. According to Buddhism, on a relative level, we should not be surprised or alarmed if the cosmic baton passed from one generation to the next feels like it has retained a few layers of grease and grime. Clearly, all of us have both personal and communal messes to clean up. But, the concept of 'original sin' is utterly foreign to Buddhism. On the ultimate level, there is no baton, no past and no future and no such thing as a generation. The only eternity is the eternity of this moment.

Examining the workings of karma is always intriguing. For example, if our great, great grandparents had not met one day a century ago, perhaps over a church dinner in some small town, we would not be here today. Likewise, for all we know, the course of history might have been drastically altered by a subtle glance between some fair damsel and her paramour, one Saturday afternoon in the Middle Ages. The ire of some angry baron on his way to assassinate a neighboring prince might have cast a shadow all the way into the 21st century, but perhaps a smile, a wink or a poetic phrase, uttered at just the right moment, averted a war. Maybe a mosquito biting the ankle of some great general cause him to lean over and scratch just as an arrow was about to strike his neck. If a miniscule insect can affect the course of a particular battle, and in turn the flow of planetary karma, imagine all the ways our lives could have turned out differently!

In this sense, the ordinary decisions we make all day, every day, have profound implications for our great-great-great grandchildren. By simply choosing to read an article on recycling instead of doing a sudoku puzzle while waiting for our dentist appointment, we might affect our legacy for a thousand years. Every time we choose meditation over television, for example, we strengthen one habitual tendency and weaken another, and our practice has an influence over our interactions with others. Such simple choices can result in an accelerated metamorphosis or cause a slowdown in the course of our spiritual growth. Every step we take slightly alters the course of our karma forever.

Of course, there are those things over which we have no dominion. For example, we cannot choose to suddenly be a foot shorter or a year younger. And while we can decide to close our eyes and go to sleep, there will come a point after which we can no longer choose to stay asleep. No matter how hard we try, it simply won't work. Likewise, if someone says the word "Eiffel", the word "Tower" flashes across our minds accompanied by an image of the Paris landmark. Such embedded associations occur without any apparent choice on our behalf. As practitioners, this seeming lack of control can be quite frustrating. We may try to focus our awareness on our breath, but find that it goes anywhere and everywhere except where we try to direct it. When we want it to stay, it wanders; when we want it to move on, it seems stuck.

Over time, however, applied conscious intention starts to make a noticeable difference. Like taming a wild horse, we find it is possible to corral our discursiveness and coax our untamed mind to don the saddle of mindfulness. Continuously walking the path of virtue reinforces virtuous habits. Effectively this means that mindfulness practices have the power to carve new neural pathways in the brain. One could say that treading the spiritual path is a process of establishing an enlightened highway in one's mind. Strolling across a moist lawn in early summer, our footprints may linger in the dew only as long as it takes the sun's heat to dry the grass. However, if we take the same route every day for a month, the soil will become compacted, the grass will have trouble growing and before long a real footpath will emerge. In the same way, neural pathways are the result of our thinking and doing the same things over and over again. The ground of enlightenment is here; we simply have to clear the underbrush and become familiar with it. It is up to us to find our way through the neurotic jungle by choosing the path of virtue over non-virtue, again and again. Each time we bring our attention back to Square One, our relationship with presence is strengthened and feels more natural. We may be discouraged by the tenacity of our old patterns as they reassert themselves like stubborn vines, but human gray matter appears to have more plasticity than was previously assumed. Studies have confirmed what the ancients have long taught, that in matters of meditation, perseverance furthers.

Our actions are guided by our views, and all too often, our views are not in accord with reality. I am reminded of an experiment whereby a team of researchers equipped a large fish tank with a glass divider down the middle. A predator species was introduced on one side of the tank with its smaller prey on the other. Naturally, the larger fish tried to attack and eat the smaller ones. However, after bashing their heads on the glass for several weeks, they eventually gave up. When the attacking behaviors had been completely extinguished, a few of the smaller fish were introduced into the side containing the larger ones. Lo and behold, no predatory behaviors were observed. A few days later the divider was removed altogether and the two species swam around in apparent harmony.

This experiment points at how the brainwashing effects of cultural, religious and political dogmas determine our world view, making it fairly easy to predict how human beings will act in any given situation. Once convinced that we 'know' something, we find it hard to 'not know' and are less inclined to openly investigate change. People born Muslim, for example, are more likely to adhere to the Muslim faith for their entire lives than they are to change religions. The same is true for Jews, Hindus,

Catholics or Buddhists. Neuropathways that we assume to accurately map reality are resistant to detours, making us quite oppositional even in the face of scientific, empirical evidence. Paradigm shifts put tremendous pressure on the mind. Changing beliefs is much harder than changing jobs or having to alter the route we take to work each morning, yet, if we fail to challenge our embedded beliefs, we will cease to evolve.

Since intellectual prowess is often skewed by the gravity of habitual responses, staying open requires that we work with our resistance. There are those who learn to meditate on a Sunday, and begin a daily practice on Monday that never falters. Most of us, however, have had to work hard to fit practice into our crowded daily routines. I know many practitioners who perpetually grapple with warming a cushion more than once a week, even after ten or twenty years. Here in America, most meditators have families, jobs, car problems, mortgages and student loans. In places like Tibet, however, there are countless stories of monks, nuns, laymen and laywomen who established themselves in remote monasteries or caves, determined to meditate in solitude for their entire lives. In cultures like ours, where monasticism is rare, such commitment is hard to find. Here, serious practice is best defined by the true value placed on presence. Consider that, in the midst of a normal workday, while some people are lost in thoughts, the keenest practitioners are secretly training themselves to return to Square One.

We might chastise or berate ourselves by asking, "Why don't we practice more? Why do we resist opening our hearts and minds? Why do we approach being in the present moment with such ambivalence or even trepidation?" For some, even the way we ask such questions arouses resistance. For others, such contemplation can trigger a move forward. We might decide that we are simply lazy, but then, maybe the term laziness is too glib. The Venerable Mingyur Rinpoche explained one aspect of resistance by rolling a piece of paper into a tube. Once we have done that, it is hard to get the paper to lie flat again. We can straighten it out with our palms, but it curls up again. So we end up having to practice flattening and smoothing it over and over. The stubbornness of the paper is similar to the resistance we encounter in our path.

When we are under the control of the emotional mind, passion trumps reason; in a logical mind, reason trumps passion. In the meditator's mind, intellect and passion are both acknowledged but we use disciplined awareness to trump resistance. When intuition and intellect combine forces, inquisitiveness is energized and we are able to get a leg up on resistance. It is our passion for the truth that leads us into nowness, or, as the Buddhists would say, "Devotion is the head of meditation."

The dialectic between opening and resistance is like two aspects of ourselves wrestling inside a huge elastic shell. If we stretch our arms to the left, our right side contracts; if we extend our legs to the right, the left side resists and so on. Struggling in this way can make the task of liberation feel hopeless, but at the same time, by exerting the right effort our muscles grow stronger and our old patterns weaken. Over time, the emotional energies wrapped up in restlessness and boredom gradually shift their allegiance to inquisitiveness. This is how we find our way. When there is nowhere else to go and nothing else to do, we finally surrender to things as they are. We concede that the best place to relax from the strain of practice is within the practice itself.

Ninety-nine raindrops out of a hundred fall on the solid concrete, but one finds its way between the cracks and, over time, little shoots of grass start to grow. Consider this: if a few blades of grass can force a concrete sidewalk to crack, ripple and eventually break apart, what might a few moments of wakefulness do?

12. Humbleness

As awareness emerges from the gravitational field of ego, any sense of self-importance and urgency evaporates into the annals of absurdity.

Some people have the devotion and perseverance to make incredible dreams come true. Occasionally, out of some small town in the middle of nowhere, a local student rises to the top of his or her class and is propelled into an elite college with the highest standards. There, with a lot of hard work, he or she achieves exceptional goals. Occasionally, such a student draws the attention of NASA and is recruited for the space program. Imagine being such a brilliant, optimistic young man or woman, fresh out of college about to enter a brilliant career with the rare chance to visit outer space!

All astronauts, male and female, undergo grueling batteries of physical, emotional and psychological testing before being selected to participate in any space shuttle mission. So, let's assume you make the grade and successfully enter the meat-grinder. For three long years, your team undergoes every kind of physical and mental ordeal. You do millions of push-ups, run endless laps, perform hundreds of underwater feats and attend thousands of classes. So many details are committed to memory and so many practice drills are repeated that you can literally do trigonometry in your sleep.

At last, the big day arrives and the mission is declared a 'go'. With the sky crystal clear and the winds light out of the south, the spacecraft is wheeled onto its launching pad. As you and your team of astronauts boards the craft for one last time, the final countdown begins. Everyone is excited and nervous. The thought crosses your mind that you may never see any of this again, but there's no turning back. This is it- T minus Six, ...Five, ...Four, ...Three, ...Two,............. BLAST OFF!

In an orgasm of light, sound, intense heat and vibration, your entire lifetime is condensed into one ecstatic, explosive thrust. Finally the spacecraft ascends into the heavens and the familiar world shrinks below. A few moments later, after the capsule sheds its thrusters, it emerges from the blue halo of the Earth's atmosphere. The entire east coast of North America is visible through one porthole. Inside the cramped module, you and your weightless crew undergo an irreversible transformation. As if a new dimension reality is being unfurled, you are struck by the sheer immensity of a horizonless eternity. Unable to utter a word, you, the quarterback, valedictorian and the pride and joy of parents, family, town, state and nation, look past the glowing earth, and suddenly you feel smaller than a mosquito in a football stadium. Having achieved what would appear to be the ultimate dream of those millions of people below, you find yourself engulfed by a profound sense of humbleness.

As awareness emerges from the gravitational field of ego, any sense of self-importance and urgency evaporates into the annals of absurdity. For a brief moment, at least, your cosmic predicament comes into perspective. And since infinite vastness leaves nothing for thoughts to cling to, your thinking mind utterly dissolves. Whenever we relax into that state of pure awe, humbleness increases and increases until the travesties of duality, of self and other, past and future and outer and inner, all fall away. Finally, we arrive in a state of true simplicity.

A warrior's spiritual trajectory does not aim at the outskirts of planetary orbit; rather it targets the inner space of this very moment. NASA astronauts may spend years in arduous preparation for some final thrust, but our spiritual careers prepare us for nowness. The great death of ego, the big moment of simply letting go, leaves us suspended in the non-dual space where watcher and watched are one. Our mission is performed over and over until we develop a heightened sense of one-pointedness and mental precision. But the big moment happens all the time. Eventually, even in our sleep we plunge into egolessness. Our meditation cushion is our space shuttle. Renunciation and devotion are the jet fuels that propel us. Our purpose is to expand our view and embrace the world with heartfelt compassion until we experience the ultimate result, which is our own dissolution.

Since the greatest breakthroughs happen when we venture outside the orbit of our egos, our greatest challenge is to transcend ego-striving altogether and surrender to a truth that is larger than our own. Traveling beyond conceptual duality is not a matter of accumulating more facts and better ideas; it is a question of letting go, of no longer identifying with what we know, or with ourselves as the knower. We launch ourselves into the space of 'not-knowing' and as we leave ego-orbit, we switch from thinking mind to listening mind and let go into the spaciousness of the present moment.

By ceasing to identify with the 'knower' we leave behind the arrogance of the opinionated self. In the language of genuine warriorship, we become truly humble or *meek*. This humbleness marks a significant stage of warriorship symbolized by a robust young tiger walking slowly and mindfully through a jungle. The young tiger has tremendous dignity. His openness and attention are clear and crisp, yet he is not dazzled by feelings of power. The warrior of meek leaves behind tendencies toward being pompous or arrogant, or for that matter, feelings of being poverty-stricken and victimized, and enters the fresh atmosphere of *suchness*. Because the tiger is content within the present moment, he is able to read the scents and odors on the breeze with respect, awe and delight. Having let go of being the expert, his mind explores the limitless universe of presence.

Such a warrior, it is said, is kind to himself and merciful to others. Confidence arises not from territoriality, but from its lack. The tiger's strength comes from his allegiance with the earth and his appreciation of basic goodness. Grounded in the essential dignity of meekness, his humbleness becomes a portal into the sacred. Without arrogance to support it, aggression is pacified. The tiger's world is seen in terms of cosmic precision, egolessness and selfless discernment. When the tiger walks on this earth, every blade of grass is worthy of appreciation and celebrated for its suchness.

13. Life and Death

Only because of the inseparability of birth and death is earthly existence tenable. While it may not seem fair, life cannot endure without death.

When the Internet was young and first began flooding the world with information, people were thrilled and intrigued. Yet, the same window that opened us up to sparkling new ideas and cutting-edge scientific developments also exposed the world's underside. Raw images of war, hunger, despair and torment were mixed in with beautiful and inspiring images of outer space and tropical islands. The great promises in innovation that began to transform how people viewed everything from graphics and design to education were offset by equally easy access to degrading pornography, violence, twisted politics and unfiltered decadence. Simultaneously, we found ourselves being catapulted toward awakening and confusion; a mile east meant a mile west at the same time. Within the unrelenting intensity of this bombardment, human evolution both imploded and exploded, all at once. The world was stretched and thrust into an unparalleled paradigm that has had some unexpected consequences.

About a month after the 9/11 attacks, I first heard the phrase "compassion fatigue" used on public radio. It had been observed that, when repeatedly exposed to the full range of peoples' traumatic narratives, otherwise kind and caring people responded with muted empathy and even mild impatience. Compassion fatigue is a sad but prevalent aspect of our communal psyche. Towards the end of 2004, as the first live news reports of the great Asian tsunami shocked the world, people were moved to tears. By the following summer, as the USA endured the record-breaking onslaught of hurricanes Katrina, Rita and Wilma, the public were still visibly affected and responded heroically but slightly less generously. However, by October of 2005, when a massive 7.6 magnitude earthquake struck Northern Pakistan, something strange and unexpected happened; the world went limp. Exhausted public and private relief agencies were increasingly challenged to raise money and support. Even as heroic journalists tramped into remote villages in a tired race to bring up-to-the-minute reports, people all over the globe sighed with a collective sense of burnout. The political will to rush to Pakistan's aid seemed lackluster. Although more than 75,000 people died and an additional 3.5 million were left homeless, this catastrophic event faded from public awareness rather abruptly.

In the end, the death toll from the Pakistani quake far surpassed that of all US disasters, including those of hurricanes and war for the previous five years combined. For compassion fatigued North Americans, however, it was just another ripple in a turbulent news year. Somewhere along the line the threshold of unbearable sadness had been crossed. Even if we tried to cry, there were just no more tears.

In the blur of the information age, the swirl of hurricanes, genocide, pandemics and earthquakes quickly become old news. Current and looming disasters are waiting in the wings to demand our attention. Worldwide financial crisis, wars in Afghanistan and Iraq, starvation in Zimbabwe and North Korea and so on, are just the most recent waves to hit the beach. There is always an endless sea of catastrophes and seemingly irresolvable and unrelenting crises brewing. As our population grows, each new headline threatens a tragedy of such staggering magnitude that our tired minds dissociate or recoil in disbelief.

Compassion fatigue is just one more sign that the revolving door into and out of the human realm is spinning at a dizzying rate. It is estimated that, on average, more than 150,000 human beings pass away while more than 325,000 are born every day. Just in the time it has taken you to read this chapter, somewhere on Earth probably 150 people have died and roughly 350 births have taken place. If this is true, and it appears to be, the world's population is growing exponentially and the pace of this onslaught is only going to get worse. No matter how fast the spent corpses of the stale and toothless are ushered out the back door, the incoming tide of fresh and toothless newbies is swamping the front entrance. During the next generation of teeth, the population of this world may double or even triple unless natural disasters and incurable diseases pick up the tempo.

Our species does not own this planet; we are simply guests and accidental custodians. The living space we occupy today has been shared by countless others throughout time. We may have inherited a paradise, but this once majestic hotel is getting crowded and run down. The banisters are frail and the pipes rattle; the carpets are threadbare and moths have eaten holes in the bedspreads. Unfortunately, we can't hang a big "No Vacancy" sign on the human realm while we undertake renovations, as much as we might like to. It is quite clear that no matter what we do, our numbers are destined to swell over the short-term, at least. Indeed, it is estimated that, by the turn of the 31st century, barring dramatic shifts in certain areas, each of us will be allotted less than one square foot of habitable space- not even enough room to lie down!

Such a vision is, of course, absurd. Nonetheless, a worldwide "claustrophobia pandemic" has already begun. And unfortunately, wherever overcrowding is a major issue, tempers tend to flare and things can get downright ugly. Because human beings are slow to adjust to this form of imbalance, xenophobia and the precursors of ethnic violence can be expected. While it may not seem fair, it is only because of the inseparability of birth and death that earthly existence is at all tenable. Indeed, life cannot endure without death. The very thought of dying may leave us feeling sad or terrified, but a dignified demise is both appropriate and ecological. If every known disease were eradicated tomorrow, the human existence would fast become a nightmare. Imagine everyone from the last ten generations all out walking their dogs with no place to go and no plans of leaving. Where would we put our "stuff"? What would we eat? And where would we find our inspiration to continue? When death knocks at our door, we should be grateful for the time we have shared, yet, be prepared to summon the courage to go forth with a sense of grace and generosity.

It seems natural to rejoice at birth and rail against death, but their delicate balancing act cannot be avoided. People don't expect to be swept out to sea by tsunamis or crushed by falling skyscrapers; we don't tuck our children in at night expecting a 4 AM mudslide, but death is certain and comes without warning. While the time and form of our demise is uncertain, ultimately our departure is inescapable. We may die tomorrow or in six months, or we may survive another sixty years, who can say? Certainly "when" may be unclear, but "if" is beyond doubt.

Death is rarely a comfortable, casual issue, but a sincere contemplation of death can ignite our determination to wake up. According to Tibetan logic, it makes more sense to plan for our next life than to plan for next year, since the next life is certain while next year is uncertain. Relating bravely with the inevitability of death should encourage us to embrace the evanescence of life. The very prospect of dying can zap us with a jolt of nowness until each moment of life contains the freshness of the entire universe. When we die, the past and the future die with us, but the present will live on. Like a spear at our backs, an awareness of death can prod us to live each nanosecond fully awake, with the attitude that there is no time to waste and no percentage in clinging to the past or future.

14. Nowness and a Sense of Humor

For the chronically serious, a deep, spontaneous belly laugh may be the next best thing to enlightenment.

For centuries, the earth was thought to be at the center of the universe while the sun and moon held sway as the ultimate god and goddess of the heavens. These two were, after all, the most brilliant and mysterious objects imaginable. For centuries, sun worship was a deadly serious business that spelled doom for unlucky virgins, goats and boars. But, as priests and shamans were forced to hone their sacrificial and ritualistic skills and gradually temper their religious beliefs with the insights of science, the sun and moon took their places in the more realistic context of a solar system and a spiral galaxy.

To this day, most gods are believed to abide 'on high' and almost all religious deities are anthropomorphic. Modernity has stripped the sun of its divinity and only sentimental poets worship the moon anymore. It is common knowledge that the lunar surface reflects rather than radiates light, and that the sun is basically a nuclear fireball. In this age of quantum mechanics and string theory, astrophysics is rarely presented in a language understood by the common man. Yet, despite their fall from pantheistic grace, these two celestial orbs have retained some grandeur. Sunsets are still glorious and the full moon is still a thing of splendor. And while the idea of making animal and human sacrifices on flaming pyres to alleviate droughts and floods does seem comical at best, and a barbaric waste of livestock and maidens at worst, we are still awed by the mysterious powers of the universe.

Over the course of time, as we have emerged from the dreamlike influences of tempestuous deities, we have grown kinder. This may be true, in part, because compared to the Middle Ages, today's sophisticated view of the cosmos actually affords us an awakened sense of humor. Human folly is not always seen as funny, particularly when we are the subject of the joke. However, the more realistic our view the more elegant our wit. If bird droppings splatter all over our windshield while we are trying to make a left turn in rush hour traffic, it is unlikely to seem very funny at the time. However, when we describe the scene later to our friends, they find it hilarious. Only when we can step back and see the whole scene within a larger context do we tend to laugh along with them.

To appreciate humor, particularly in the context of the communal insanity of the human race, we need a lot of spaciousness. Humor opens a relief valve that allows a more cosmic perspective and stimulates the flow of fresh air. It reminds us that today's absolute certainties may be tomorrow's primitive beliefs and dislodges the stagnancy of fixation. When weighed down by habitual patterns, it is easy to become uptight, superstitious, despondent or defeatist. So when we feel like we are not getting anywhere on our spiritual journey, we usually need to lighten up. A little humor can go a long way in giving us a fresh outlook and the space to breathe.

Viewing the earth from the sun or moon's perspective might provide levity on a grander scale. For one thing, concepts like 'last year' or 'tomorrow' might start to seem meaningless. In the vastness of space, the sun rests in eternal immediacy. Space itself never sets, never rises and never goes anywhere. It's only down here on earth, where every month we have to pay our bills and every morning we have to eat our breakfasts, that space and time seem solid. From the perspective of the moon or the sun, if a little dust settles on our dresser, it doesn't need to cause jaw-grinding urgency. Life's duties can be performed within the spaciousness of a sense of humor.

When we adopt a more spacious view, our clenched fists open and we can see the uptightness of our demands as extensions of our egos. A lack of humor can turn the practice of mindfulness on its head. Instead of relaxing into presence, we are seduced into stoicism. Practice becomes a race to finish a prescribed number of mantras or complete the next round of trainings at some frantic pace. Secretly competing with others, we forget that the point is to develop patience and let go. Hoping to eventually become a teacher, we study to perform rituals with dazzling dexterity, only to become immune to genuine feedback along the way. Rather than rejoicing in the insights of others, we become jealous. The longer we have been around our particular scene, the more spiritual cachet we feel we should command. Sometimes we become maniacal when slighted and cast harsh judgment on those who practice other paths or unleash resentment on those fortunate enough to go on retreat while we are left doing the grunt work of cleaning up after a class. Even monks and nuns have been known to scrap over access to their teacher like dogs fighting over meat. "How come I still have to continue to let go?" each one wonders discreetly. "After all, haven't I been through the whole renunciation thing five times already? It just doesn't seem fair!" Yet the more serious our indignation, the more important a sense of humor becomes.

It may be useful to remember *Nature's Third Law of Cosmic Humor*: "*Those who cling to the ridiculousness of ego can expect a pie in the face from time to time.*"

For those serious about developing wakefulness, confirmation of ego is never the point. And thank goodness for that! The pie that hits us in the smacker contains a very important message. It tells us that the peace we have been searching for throughout the universe has been right in front of our nose all along. Meanwhile, the 'self' that we have taken as the central reference point for our existence is nowhere to be found! Meditators have been prominently featured in the punch line of this scenario for centuries. Those who can laugh gain the smile of realization; those who can't remain solidified and bear the pathetic frown of the insulted.

Ultimately, we all have to relate to the cosmic joke sooner or later. For the chronically serious, a deep, spontaneous belly laugh may be the next best thing to enlightenment. And, to add to the irony, when our practice needs a good broadside, we are unlikely to see it coming. Yet inevitably, some cosmic trickster sweeps down on us disguised as a critical life event that nudges us in the ribs perfectly on cue. Hopefully, we have enough presence to drop our convoluted storylines and chuckle.

Milarepa, the great Tibetan saint, was once tormented by incessant thoughts in the form of demons. Recognizing that he was caught in the trap of seriousness, he sang a song comparing a yogi who cannot relax into basic being to a fish that cannot swim, or a bird that cannot fly. As he mocked his own pretentiousness, the obstructing demons vanished. A Zen master might invite us to tame the self by forgetting the self. Some wrathful Hindu yogi might continually poke us in the ribs to make us smile. Maybe our compassionate lama refuses our request for an interview to undermine a subtle dependency. All these interactions are intended to invite humor into the student's perspective.

Trungpa Rinpoche encouraged his students to leap into space over and over again. He once told a story about a poor fellow who was so depressed that he was considering suicide. Sitting in his lonely kitchen one evening, he really felt he had reached the end of his rope. He was so bereft of optimism that, seeing no point in going on, he took a fading flower and placed it in a solitary vase. When it ceremoniously drooped at just the right angle, he took it as a sign and composed a poetic note of understated pathos. When he felt he had found exactly the right words, he propped his little poem against the vase, and placed a half-consumed glass of red wine nearby. Finally, with an eternal sigh, he pulled a hood over his eyes, pried open the window and climbed out on to the ledge. With a drum roll mounting inside his chest, he took a deep breath, leaned forward and leapt. "I believe it was then," Rinpoche would chuckle, "that he remembered he lived in a ground floor apartment."

15.   Meeting the Mullah

Finally, his mind's motor seemed to run out of gas and he just fell silent, inside and out. It didn't matter what thoughts came and went through his mind, he was just there.

Years ago, while traveling in southern Morocco, I met a man in a small café on the edge of the Sahara Desert. He had just returned from a Sufi monastery rumored to be home to an enlightened abbot and his adventure illuminates the strange turns the warrior's path can take.

It was the early 1970's and travel in that part of the world was not easy. Just finding a caravan going in the right direction was a challenge and any surety of being delivered to one's destination was a bonus. Nonetheless, this fellow made contact with the right people and after three or four days of hard travel through dusty dunes and vast expanses, a small herd of trucks bore him, along with a few Arab traders, to the middle of nowhere. The famous 'monastery' he had hoped to find turned out to be a humble compound of dusty tents and semi-permanent structures near a small oasis.

Undaunted, and glad to be off the back of the truck, he maintained an optimistic mood. It was early morning and it seemed as if the whole 'village' of fifty or more people had turned out to greet him. The first order of business was to secure lodging, so he made arrangements to stay in a local tea shanty. In broken Arabic, my friend tried to explain that he had come from a long way away to meet a famous Mullah. His host shrugged and pointed to the Sufi compound, not more than a few hundred yards away.

As he approached the gate, he was greeted by a thin, toothless man who showed him to a small tent housing nothing but a small bench and an awning with flaps that could be adjusted for shade. Like every other structure in the neighborhood, it provided an unencumbered view of the wide-open Sahara.

My friend spent the rest of that first day in that quiet tent alone looking out at distant dunes and rehearsing what he would say when presented to the Mullah. Periodically the older man would look in on him, which my friend took as a reassuring sign. But when asked about the Mullah, the old man simply gestured to him to sit and wait. Assuming this was standard protocol, my friend silently complied.

However, before long the heat waves dancing off the immensity of the landscape began to have an effect on him. Being somewhat restless and tired, he felt a need to stand up and stretch, walk a little or nod off for a while. By the time the sun neared the horizon, he noticed that it was amazingly quiet. The trucks had all left and the men of the compound were moving about like zephyrs when he heard the familiar call to pray at the mosque. Not being a Muslim, my friend did not attend but rather settled into his own meditation practice. It felt good to be alone and still.

The peace of the late afternoon helped relieve the sense of irritability that had begun to creep over him. He sensed that his mind was still unsettled from his trip and was relieved that his meeting with the Mullah would have to wait until the next day.

The remote settlement could hardly be called a village. Apart from some scattered tents, there was a cluster of six mud walled buildings and a smattering of cardboard hovels. As the next caravan was not scheduled to arrive for two weeks, this would be his home for the next fortnight. The tea merchant, his patron, seemed very content to have company, but due to language issues, there was little conversation, and after a brief walk under the amazing canopy of the desert sky, he fell asleep.

In the morning, he arose feeling refreshed, stretched, shared some tea, a few biscuits and fractured bits of conversation with his host. Then he made his way back to the shade tent with much anticipation, but with no sign of the Mullah, or anyone else for that matter, he simply took his seat and began to watch his breath. Only after the second *Adhan*, or call to prayer, and after the hot sun was well above the horizon, did the old servant surface. He dropped into the tent bearing a half-full teapot, a smile and some biscuits, seemingly amused that this Englishman, who spoke almost no Arabic, should be sitting on a bench in the middle of the desert in the morning heat. After awhile, they dispensed with the bench and sat on a carpet spread on the ground.

My friend later described this fellow as part gracious host, part prison warden. Always warm, but sometimes very stern, the old man had an uncanny way of turning up just when my friend was falling asleep or felt the need to stand up and stretch his legs. Somehow, they managed to communicate. With no telephones, no electricity and only one small well, the village and the compound were something out of a timeless era. The only way in or out was with the convoy of trucks that passed through on certain market days, or perhaps by joining up with some tribal Bedouins who would amble by on camels. But desert people had few firm deadlines or clear destinations. So my friend was cornered, or so it seemed.

So, with a full two weeks of nothing to do but sit and wait, my friend tried to settle in to his hot and dusty predicament. He had never been anywhere so excruciatingly boring. As the minutes became hours, and mornings melted seamlessly into endless afternoons, he just sat, breathing the sandy air. Almost always alone, almost always looking out at the barren dunes, he wondered how long it would take him to go mad.

During the first few days he would marvel at how many tricks his mind could play on itself. At different points, he was completely convinced that he saw lakes, rivers, people and animals and whole caravans that would never arrive. He was shocked that his mind could construct elaborate advancing armies, so real he feared for his life. He saw camel herds and dancing women, airplanes, cities and tornadoes, all of them mere hallucinations. But, alas, no Mullah! "Just as well!" he thought, for at times, he was convinced that he had indeed gone crazy. Other times, staring out into the intensity of the bright sand, he felt a profound sense of freedom and relief. Then paradoxically, the enormity of the open space would produce a sense of intense claustrophobia. Time and again, just as he was about to break down in tears, the old man would pass by with more tea and biscuits and a radiant toothless smile.

However, as sand found its way into absolutely every pore of his skin, his hope of ever meeting the famous Mullah faded. A flood of new obsessions replaced the old. He became critically concerned with water, food and his own mental health. As the residents of the compound silently passed by, he imagined them snickering and mocking him. What a fool to have come all this way for nothing! Or worse, traveling thousands of miles just to be scorned! He felt naked and vulnerable, but actually, they did not seem to find his presence all that unusual. To them he was just the latest in a line of westerners, all of whom were inexplicably strange.

With endless time to think, he pondered his life back in Europe. He daydreamed of lovers, family and friends and revisited every relationship, job, class and picnic of his childhood. He imagined making amends with those he had harmed and envisioned thanking his professors in school for their kindness. He pictured the streets where he grew up with his aunts and uncles and cousins. Every poem, every story and every film he could recall was recited and replayed until he had exhausted himself. Then he turned to the future and planned the next fifty years. Finally, his mind's motor seemed to run out of gas and he just fell silent, inside and out. It didn't matter what thoughts came and went through his mind, he was just there. So with nothing to do but sit and breathe and look out into the desert sky, he began to settle.

From that point, when the old man ambled by, he simply returned his nod and smiled with a sense of defeat. One day, as the old man poured some tea but said nothing, he solemnly placed his hand on my friend's shoulder. For a moment, like two old friends, they just sat together in deep silence. It all felt so ordinary. Then, the old man picked up his things and whispered, "Sahib, be patient. You see Mullah tomorrow for sure!"

As his two week stay was drawing to an end, he noticed a definite shift in the energy of the compound. So what if the long-awaited truck caravan was coming to his rescue the next day. So what if the reclusive Mullah had still not taken pity on him! My friend had lost all sense of urgency. Maybe he was mildly excited about the arrival of the caravan, but the little shade tent had become his home and he would miss the daily ritual of just sitting and sipping tea. The scorching dessert heat had burned away his cynicism, and cleansed him of defeat and even boredom. He had exhausted all fascination with the past or future. Somewhere along the line, he had relinquished the need for answers from Holy Men. Ironically, he had stopped complaining just in time to leave.

An hour after sunrise, a column of dust was spotted on the horizon. As ten large, loud, diesel trucks pulled in from the dessert and ground to a noisy halt, the village became as animated and chaotic as it had been the day of his arrival. Immediately, my friend was swept up in the furor. He haggled with a driver and reserved his place on one of the trucks and went to gather up his few belongings. He had long forgiven the old servant for his master's lack of hospitality but was still intrigued by his comments from the previous day. So, knowing he would be gone in less than an hour, he tried to find the old man.

He returned to his shade tent and waited, but when the old man did not show up, he became concerned. The caravan would be leaving soon. He looked everywhere he could think of and asked everyone he met, but no one had seen the old fellow. He bowed his goodbyes to each of the acolytes and settled things with the owner of the teashop. But still no sign of the old man! Finally a young initiate motioned to my friend to follow him into the back of a large tent at the edge of the monastic compound. There, behind a decorative partition, he could hear men laughing.

In the midst of a group of truck drivers sat the old servant, smiling, smoking a cigarette and enjoying some mint tea. He saw my friend and motioned for him to enter the circle. The old man took one of my friend's hands and held it in his own and, in Arabic, apparently explained to the truck drivers all about my poor friend's desire to meet the great Mullah. They all appeared solemn for a moment, but then all at once the tent broke out in a roar of spontaneous laughter. One driver turned and, in perfect English, asked, "So, my friend, what do you think of the famous Mullah now?"

My friend explained that he didn't know what to say, since they hadn't really met. Again, everyone roared in laughter and slapped their knees. Finally, the driver turned to the secretary and said, "Mullah, with all due respect, it's time we were on our way." All the men rose, kissed the hands of the old servant, and bowed as they received his blessing. My friend was left alone with the Mullah for the last time.

Apparently, he cried for about five minutes with a deep muscular sobbing that seemed to rumble from the pit of his empty stomach. Then, after crying, he started to laugh. And the Mullah laughed as well. The two men laughed so hard that their eyes and faces hurt. They laughed and cried until there were no more tears. Finally, everything became silent and they just sat in complete stillness. My friend described the feeling as falling into the infinite space between joy and sadness. He felt as if his mind had been stripped naked and bathed with a love beyond words like nothing he had ever felt before.

Finally the Mullah signaled it was time to leave. My friend recalls that he laughed and cried intermittently for several days on the back of the truck that carried him back to the coast and civilization. He had been back two weeks by the time I met him and had only begun to share his story with a few people. Tears still formed as he spoke. It was the only time we ever met and I don't remember his name. But I remember his eyes.

16. The Tender Heart of Sadness

Simply stated, when we focus our energy on the present moment and engage the power of our hearts, our connection to reality is amplified.

When the charge of life hits us smack in the face, we could rejoice. After all, every genuine arousal presents us with an opportunity to rediscover the potency of awareness. And since the warrior's path is about working with power, we should expect to occasionally wake up to a world shimmering with intensity. Like it or not, we live in a brilliant and dynamic universe where no holds are barred and even hurricanes and tornadoes are fair play. But such vividness comes at a price; we have to give up our complaints about the cards we are dealt and step outside our comfort zones. To taste the naked power of things as they are, we need to seize each moment.

Warriors are not intimidated by power. Just as a stunning piece of art can communicate the rawness of emotions, blasts of non-conceptual perception can transmit the freshness of first thought. We should welcome such flashes with delight. Second thoughts and third thoughts are just aftershocks or commentaries. If we happen to set out on a clear, dark evening to walk the dog and look up just in time to see a brilliant shooting star streaking across the heavens, our hearts soar. We know the sky is not falling, but beyond that we need no explanation. We can accept the immensity and brilliance of the universe leaping out at us with humble awe. It is invigorating to be reminded that nothing is static and that even space is electric.

As practitioners, we have little choice but to meet the world on its own terms. We can hardly invite in the majesty of the phenomenal world and then rescind the gesture. When we open the doors and let the wind blow in, we can expect to have our chains rattled, to be poked, prodded or jostled by whatever it takes to keep us awake. And once we fully commit to the warrior's way, we are fair game. Our spiritual alarm clocks are permanently set to go off at a moment's notice with no snooze button. Indeed, only when all avoidance options are taken off the table can we fully embrace our fiercest fears.

When we embrace our fears, instead of squirming to withdraw inside our cocoons, true fearlessness dawns. A virtuous commitment to presence inspires the dignified posture of royalty. So, we might imagine ourselves seated on the throne of the eternal moment flanked by those fearless warriors of the past, present and future whose commitment to presence is unshakeable. One way or another, we will be confirmed and supported if we genuinely contemplate the Great Eastern Sun. The feeling of good head and shoulders extends into every pore of our body and beyond, out into the world. As if riding a galloping steed, we are launched into the field of nowness over and over again, challenging ourselves to open our hearts further and further and unleash our presence as it radiates out into the universe.

Lungta is a Tibetan word that literally means *'wind horse'*. It refers to the inner vibrancy that is summoned when we no longer repress the power within our hearts. It is the confidence of fearlessness, the passion of gentleness and the incorruptible power of wakefulness, all bundled together in a unified display of dazzling authenticity. I think of sunlight striking a proud maple on an early summer morning. As the highest leaves and branches begin to glow in the sunrise, they communicate with the roots deep in the earth. One can sense the flowing sap, the leaves rustling in the breeze, the trunk exuding strength and the entire tree buzzing with life. Like a conduit between heaven and earth, devoid of apology, complaint or any sense of poverty, the tree almost becomes a deity, personifying the summer's richness. When we fully embody presence without ambivalence, we exude lungta just like that majestic maple. By simply being, without any leaks, cracks or inadequacies, our bodies and minds synchronize and heaven and earth are joined.

When accomplished musicians perform with lungta, their hearts soar and the audience is swept along for the ride. When a figure skater skates with lungta, gliding as effortlessly as a gust of wind across a frozen pond and leaping into a double axel that defies gravity, we gasp in awe. I am sure each of us, at some time or other, has felt the power of our own personal brilliance. All the world's great spiritual and cultural traditions appreciate that magic. They value lungta as the fundamental basis of individual and societal well-being. The Maori warriors of the South Pacific perform the *haka*, a windhorse raising ritual that practically explodes with potency. Indigenous tribes from the Pacific Northwest have slightly similar dances. People from all parts of the globe employ communal rites, fire practices or other rituals to sew the sacred and the practical aspects of their lives together. Rousing lungta unifies the individual with the forces of the natural world and empowers the heart. Simply stated, when we focus our energy on the present moment and engage the power of our hearts, our connection to reality is amplified.

When we rouse lungta we become like fully charged batteries: strong, awake and radiant with the life force of confidence. Raising lungta cuts through fixation and transcends aggression, allowing us to harness the power of immediacy. When authentic lungta fills our beings we can't avoid the tender sadness of our own hearts. In fact, our intimate relationships with ourselves become beacons of confidence for the rest of the world.

When we speak of a tender heart of sadness, we are not referring to melancholy or mundane disappointment. A warrior's sadness has little in common with the emotional deflation, depression or self-pity normally associated with the word sadness. Rather, the 'genuine heart of sadness' borders on joy. Trungpa Rinpoche called it *"the ideal human emotion"*. When our longing for sanity melts into an appreciation of sacredness, it leaves us tenderized, transports us to the frontiers of intimacy and invites us to leap. It is one thing to talk about the power of the human heart, but another to step bravely forward and taste its fragile essence.

Trungpa Rinpoche said, *"Fear does not allow fundamental tenderness to enter into us. When tenderness tinged by sadness touches our heart, we know that we are in contact with reality. We feel it. That contact is genuine, fresh, and quite raw. That sensitivity is the basic experience of warriorship."* So our challenge is to meet fear with fearlessness and aggression with tenderness. This kind of relationship with power creates an atmosphere of unrequited love, non-conceptual bravery and vulnerability that is quite literal and tangible.

Imagine yourself standing on a rocky ledge overlooking a vast canyon when suddenly from out of nowhere a hawk soars into view. Riding effortlessly on an updraft, the majestic bird is thrust into the center of your field of vision and suspended, just for a second, in mid-air not more than twenty feet away. You can taste the bird's power and splendor as clearly as if you shared its wings. Suddenly, its feathered head turns and its noble your eyes meet your own. Neither of you flinch. Time stands utterly still and an indescribable energy arcs across the gap between you. Then, with an imperceptible flex of a wing, it drops out of view and is gone. You are left feeling utterly naked, as if your heart had been sliced open.

When the phenomenal world calls us to attention, we respond from a place of timeless presence. Waves of lungta swell within us, a spontaneous fever of love and compassion fills our hearts and there is a stillness that bears the stamp of eternity. Sadly, such intimacy can't be shared. We are so alone that we do not even have ourselves to keep us company.

17. The Eternally Youthful Mind

Whether we are physically strong or weak, happy or sad, smart or dull, our common denominator as human beings will always be the miracle of present consciousness.

When we are young, it is virtually impossible to imagine how it really feels to grow old. Yet, if we live long enough, our skin will eventually wrinkle and our posture will sag. We will lose our teeth, parts of our memory and our keen eyesight, and in general, suffer all kinds of limitations. One way or another, we are sure to evolve into miserable, cranky old farts, kind and gentle elders or some combination thereof. Seldom do we realize that the decisions we make in our twenties will cast long shadows into our eighties. As young people, life has caprice. We think of ourselves as either lucky or unlucky victims of circumstance, somehow divorced from the natural consequences of our impulses. Once we embrace a regimen of practice, however, that sense of randomness starts to shift and we discover we can exert more and more dominion over our actions. Thus, by engaging in genuine spirituality, we consciously set the course of our own maturation. We become managers of our karmic accounts, able to choose to invest in dharmic actions, (those that bring wisdom, joy and contentment), or we can continue to gamble on materialism and live at the mercy of uncertain dividends.

As long as we cast ourselves as random pinballs set loose in a chaotic universe, we will remain slaves to what feels like a predestined spiritual fate. But if we awaken to the profound karmic opportunity represented by a life of practice, we can joyfully accept the burden of rational choice. In either case, we cannot escape the laws of cause and effect. Although the details of karma are infinitely complex, the basics are quite simple: we reap what we sow. And, since karmic seeds require the soil of outer conditions, we should be aware of the dangers of stewing in negative emotions and associating with those who consistently harbor a bitter and resentful outlook. Throughout our lives we need to choose the higher path of intelligence, appreciation, intuition and clarity, over the lower road of deceit, complaint, anger, jealousy and depression. If our old age is to be a season of bountiful harvest, it is important to cultivate the right crops all along.

Although social imperatives drive us to accumulate wealth, fame, power and knowledge, we cannot afford to succumb to their allure and lose our focus. While such pursuits are not entirely antithetical to warriorship, they can be huge distractions. The heroism of the heart has less to do with achieving a radiant physique, stunning intellect or an overflowing retirement account and more to do with wearing out ego.

As aging warriors we become experts at falling apart. Thus, throughout our lives our choices should lead us into the realm of humbleness rather than arrogance. That way, we are less likely to sag under the weight of our own accumulated karma and more likely to rise up on the basis of accumulated merit. We learn to value simple virtues rather than thirst for power over others. Whenever our 'trip' is exposed or we are caught in ego's web of neurotic subterfuge, we can take it as a cue to surrender, reset our moral compass and clean up our mess without repairing or defending ourselves from insult. We can even be happy, knowing we have lightened our load.

If we wear out a pair of shoes, small pebbles might work their way into our socks through a torn seam. If we continue wearing the same shoes, eventually our toes might come in touch with the actual sidewalk. Of course, we are unlikely to let things go that far before buying a new pair. However, as we rub up against the Dharma and our old patterns become increasingly threadbare, we should resist the inclination to replace one neurotic habit with another. The more we practice, the less we feel a need to defend and repair our broken reputations. After all, we have worked hard to exhaust our ego and its delusions, so why work against the process.

Having led a number of month-long group meditation retreats, I have enjoyed the privilege of observing hosts of angry, tough, leathery egos decay and unravel. Mindfulness has a powerful reversing effect on egoic tendencies, such as the impulse to shut down. It is wonderful to see stark rigidity give way to inquisitive suppleness in the intensified atmosphere of group practice, where the work of staying open always brings interesting and satisfying results. Bit by bit, the attention habitually dedicated to shoring up defenses is liberated into presence. As hours turn into days, people's hard edges soften like ice cream left in the sun.

Longer retreats afford us the time to experiment with deeper levels of relaxation. We are often surprised by how much stronger our hearts feel after hours of sitting up straight, bringing our minds back to the present moment and letting go. The willingness to be with our sadness and tenderheartedness without running away seems to create firmer, more genuine handshakes and warmer, more authentic hugs. By relating to our own depths, we gain the confidence to look into each other's eyes. As fear, pain and awkwardness evaporate into the mist, we are left with nonjudgmental empathy. What we are uncovering is actually the eternal youthfulness of the present moment.

Imagine being able to share our eyes with a blind person, even just for an hour! What a remarkable gift that would be! Imagine how someone who lives forever in darkness would look at even the most simple and ordinary things of this world - a ceiling tile, a decaying leaf, a drop of water by the sink! Especially knowing they had only sixty short minutes to take it all in- they would hardly want to blink. In the same way, we might find ourselves cherishing every moment! We forget the preciousness of present moment awareness because it is with us all the time. Nobody does life justice by taking things for granted. This now is the fountain of eternal youth. There can never be a future now, a better now, an older now or a younger now. There is just this now- this fleeting moment- the only seat of true joy. Whether young or old, strong or weak, happy or sad, smart or dull, our common denominator as human beings will always be the miracle of present consciousness.

Whether we are five or ninety-five years old, nowness will always be fresh and youthful. We may regret having wasted our formative years, but although they are gone, we still have this moment. We may anticipate bright or dim prospects, but that future will never arrive. Instead, we will remain stuck right here in the middle of time where it is neither too late nor too early to wake up. Our dreams can only happen right now. In this dream, no matter where we are along the spectrum of decay, we can celebrate our life with an ever-fresh wakefulness that transcends age.

Repeatedly practicing the fine art of sitting still and letting go is like holding a magnifying glass- the light streams in and concentrates awareness until consciousness burns holes in both the future and the past. Our storylines scatter and our grudges evaporate. With an eternally youthful and inquisitive outlook, we can take a childlike delight in watching things fall apart, change, reform and fall apart all over again. This sense of wonder puts us in touch with our soft spot and binds us to a world of magic.

Once, after a long retreat, I attended a stunning modern dance performance at Dartmouth College. I had just spent several weeks alone in a small cabin in the woods where things were very simple and natural, so the lights and designs of the costumes, the swirling colors, the music and the dancers' figures had a slightly overwhelming effect on me. Nonetheless, I was moved by the way everything fit together with a kind of abstract appreciation that is hard to articulate. It seemed as if a subtle tuning fork had been struck deep inside my heart and begun to resonate at a frequency that could shatter my ribcage. The performance reverberated with both a bold exuberance and a kind of softness that defied logic. Once that tuning fork began vibrating, I was rendered speechless.

Emotions associated with nowness are not self-referential, but have unique energy fields all their own. Like musical notes sung with perfect pitch, they penetrate our defenses and evoke words and silences without being trapped in either. The sublime nuances of art and music that tap into such resources become portals into a timeless, inner realm of wisdom. As we mature, our relationships with the emotions are refined. In our youth we may have had the stamina to stay up all night and dance, but as we move into the twilight years, we gain the capacity to sit perfectly still and listen to a Beethoven sonata.

Just as a sunrise or a sunset is not one thing but a concert of continually changing hues, if we try to separate day from night or even birth from death, we find we cannot.

No single event can contain the present moment, yet every breath is a unique expression of nowness. When we settle in to Square One, our lives become masterpieces that mock the very concept of time.

18. Great Eastern Sun

Working with the notion of the Great Eastern Sun encourages us to burn away the clouds of doubt and appreciate the vastness of our potential.

Opening the heart is not about words. Beautiful ideas and expressions often pay homage to a world that is emotionally vast and intellectually profound, but a reliance on words means reality is still being filtered through the windows of the thinking mind. The complete elimination of these filters is the goal of genuine spiritual discipline. Effective meditation practice is a matter of subjectively disrobing, layer by layer, until at some point, we are so utterly naked that sheer immediacy supplants concepts and ideas. Words dissolve and what fills the space between thoughts is mere presence itself.

As we approach absolute sincerity, the very language of perception changes. A flash of insight perks us up in the middle of a dull meeting and, before we utter a word, we feel a breeze of delight. Walking across the parking lot, the smell of rain slows us down. Brief flashes of nowness leverage our self-absorbed moods and relieve us of our daily burdens. Each moment that we spend back at Square One we shed another pound of angst. Like someone walking through a dark field in a thunderstorm, we no longer muddle about in the dim light of speculation but re-establish our bearings based on flashes of brilliance.

Gradually, as the brief dots of clear awakening begin to connect, a kind of spiritual photosynthesis is triggered. After repeated glimpses of our wakeful potential, we feel strangely naked and alive. The Great Eastern Sun has infiltrated the privacy of our consciousness and the path of stabilizing awareness unfolds before us. We move toward the warmth with the guidance of a genuine teacher like a bud turning towards to the midday sun. Once this process begins, there is really no turning back. The seemingly rock-hard bulb at the end of a tender vine cannot reverse its fate; having been bathed in sunlight, it has no choice but to soften. As the tight fist of petals begins to unfurl, all that is necessary is relaxation. We might be tempted to impatiently tear away the outer sheath, but once activated, the blossoming naturally runs its course.

A good gardener will make sure that her plants are properly situated, appropriately nourished, adequately watered and protected. Likewise, through daily sitting practice, study and exposure to authentic teachers, we become our own gardeners. We support our own ripening, growth and stabilization. For example, when we undergo an unexpected trauma or a disturbing life event, we take proper care of ourselves, aware that a deep spiritual response may have been triggered. Maybe our antennae pick out the meditators in the crowd or we seek the counsel of a trusted spiritual friend. One way or another, we take refuge in the best sanity available to us and find our way back to Square One.

At one time I was involved in arranging the rental of some college dormitories for a major Buddhist gathering. On Wednesday, I attended a meeting with Jim, the kitchen manager, who was in charge of food services. Jim struck me as a cordial fellow, although a little speedy. In between barking instructions to two assistants and keeping his eye on a pot of simmering soup, he presented me with price lists and explained menu options. On the whole, we made a good start but it was obvious that he was distracted and that we would have to sit down together the following Monday. Two days later Jim went home, ate something at an outdoor barbeque, and died.

As he was collapsing on his lawn, an ambulance was called. Within minutes, a crew of emergency medical technicians was administering CPR. By this time, Jim was reportedly floating above the scene in a calm state of suspended awareness. On the way to the hospital, the medics observed little to no pulse. As they rushed his limp form into the emergency room, his disembodied mind was enjoying timeless peace and blissful rapture. Later, he was able to accurately describe the movements of friends and family from the moment he was discovered lying on the ground until a voice told him that he would have to return to his body. When Jim 'woke up' on a gurney in a recovery room, he was already a different person.

Needless to say, I was quite surprised to be greeted that Monday by a warm smile and an enthusiastic hug. Physically, he appeared to be the same man I had met the week before but the resemblance stopped there. This Jim was calm and radiant. Rather than seeming rushed, he appeared to have all the time in the world. He looked me straight in the eye and emanated a spacious glow tinged with a genuine sense of concern. He had a sparkling sense of humor and would stop talking just to listen to a bird chirping. The quality of his genuineness uplifted everyone. In the course of our discussion, I asked him if he was now afraid of dying and he smiled with confidence. "No! Not at all!" he said, "In fact, we should all live our lives to the fullest, but never fear our demise!" Although it was obvious that he was being afforded a wider berth than usual by some of his more skeptical colleagues, I totally enjoyed our time together.

Near death experiences, while very dramatic, are only one among many portals into a vaster view of life. The powerful metaphor of the Great Eastern Sun, as used in the Shambhala tradition, offers us a gentler way to access the inherent brilliance of our own minds. Working with the notion of the Great Eastern Sun encourages us to burn away our clouds of doubt and appreciate the vastness of our potential. When we contemplate the image of the sun boldly illuminating the sky, the sacredness of things as they are, we are encouraged to venture beyond our ambivalence. When the first rays of the rising sun strike the tops of distant snowcapped peaks, the world is caught in transition. Everything we see and all that we feel intuitively echoes the emergence of primordial confidence. Crisp, clear morning air creates an atmosphere of unfettered communication and the majesty of the horizon against the vivid blue sky hits us like a monk striking a gong. As we invoke such images, we naturally tune in to the energy and courage of our awakened hearts.

After a good night's sleep, it is interesting to pause and tune into the dawning of our ordinary awareness. Just as the morning light strikes our eyelids, with eyes still shut, we can observe the mental shift from being asleep and dreaming to being present and awake. What is the criteria we use to determine that we are no longer dreaming? What is this different quality of our minds that blossoms all of a sudden?

If we can stay present within that organic shift of attention, the image of the rising sun takes on a very personal meaning. Surrendering our dreams, yet not rushing into our thought patterns, orients us to the sunrise of consciousness. This is the dawn of the **Great East**. By relaxing, yet remaining aware, it is possible to feel the **Sun** of presence spreading in our body and mind as a rising tide of spaciousness. As our eyes open, we can take the time to appreciate the freshness of seeing and the magic of hearing. As the flow of natural intelligence rises into our senses, just by staying present and inquisitive, we can feel our hearts beat with that fundamental quality of being that is neither 'good' nor 'bad'. **East** is the direction of the sunrise, which in this case, means the sunrise of consciousness. We 'orient' ourselves to that arising mind of living presence. The East is **Great** because relating to the vastness and power of immediacy leaves no room for the pettiness of ego. So, by tuning in to the **Great Eastern Sun,** we feel the sacredness of awareness deepen and we let go into nowness. With a willingness to celebrate the world beyond the cocoon, such warriors of the Great Eastern Sun begin their day with dignity.

19. The Setting Sun

When our dreams crumble, we suffer; yet when our delusions collapse we are set free.

Certainly we live in "interesting times", the kind referred to in the ancient Chinese curse. Fears of global warming, natural disasters, pandemics and wars have infiltrated our communal subconscious. Our hopes for a happy future are continually diminished and uncertainty is widespread. Islands are sinking, sea levels are rising, icebergs and glaciers are melting and no one is sure if the robins will return next spring. Even without tornadoes and hurricanes, daily accounts of job losses and our own financial insecurities remind us that even a modest lifestyle can be swept away in a momentary flash flood. According to the Shambhalian view, when catastrophic projections of devastation, negativity and depression dominate the minds of the population, that society has entered a Dark Age.

In this atmosphere of doom and gloom we might turn off our televisions, cancel our newspapers, shutter our windows and lock our doors. After that, we might pull the blankets over our heads, curl into a fetal position and close our eyes. However, apart from being ineffective, such gestures express the opposite of human dignity. This world does not need more cowardice, cynicism and complaint. Our appetite for an enlightened vision is not served by the fading glow of civility. In these dark times, we must remain loyal to the spirit of *bodhicitta* and seek refuge in reality as the basis for brave and compassionate action. As a society, we cannot afford to be lazy. Despite the setting sun epidemic overwhelming us, the light in our hearts must never be extinguished. The painful waning of basic goodness should be our call to action. We need to rouse ourselves and move forward, not out of fear and neurosis, but on the basis of the profound, brilliant, just, powerful, all-victorious vision of the Great Eastern Sun.

Remembering the old adage, "What were once our vices are now our habits!" many of us quietly mourn the loss of the magical world of youth or the elegance of a bygone era. Where we once enjoyed pasturelands and forests, we now endure strip malls and fast food restaurants. The sacred oceans that once teemed with an endless diversity of marine life are slowly becoming barren expanses pocked by floating mountains of septic garbage. Aggression is rapidly replacing gentleness as a social norm. The crushing burden of institutional greed and corruption has broken our backs and sent entire national economies down the slippery slope toward bankruptcy. Children fear being gunned down in the hallways of their schools and worshippers are wary of their churches and mosques. Whatever dralas we once associated with our peaceful towns and cities have sadly dispersed. Clearly, if ever there was a time for compassionate concern, this is that hour.

Films, music and even children's toys have become agents of this insidious trend. The constant zaps, blips and sub-auditory zings that have found their way into our subliminal food chain are like plankton feeding the whale-like appetite of the beast. We have certain receptors in our brains that are so over-excited that without a daily fix of loud noises and thrills, we feel painfully bored. Seeking to 'be in the moment' due to dopamine addiction is a poor substitute for wakefulness. And as a consequence of our own setting sun tendencies, our children begin life with an increased risk for anxiety, substance abuse and mood disorders. Considering how their playthings and entertainments compete with each other for brutality, shock value and explosions per minute, we hardly need to look up from our glowing screens to feel the shadows of the setting sun engulfing us.

Nonetheless, we do need to look up, take note and respond in a principled manner. As we launch our various initiatives, the fearlessness and confidence we bring to each task must be based in clear seeing. Therefore, if we are to truly benefit others, we can't avoid meditation practice. As formidable as the forces of the setting sun are, and they do have great momentum, they lack the power of genuine wisdom and compassion. If we are serious about creating an enlightened society, these are the areas in which we must concentrate our efforts.

When guided by basic goodness, as described in the Shambhala teachings, we make wiser and braver choices. Shambhala warriors are taught that even in the midst of chaos, it is critical to remain loyal to one's inherent sanity. Outwardly, our lives, our ambitions and our love affairs may be reduced to rubble, but we can always return to the basic goodness of this present moment. Our inner commitment to the sacredness of the world around us and to the dralas of the Great Eastern Sun is not negotiable. If we allow this view to infiltrate every aspect of our lives, we will naturally strengthen our primordial confidence. When things seem overwhelming, outwardly we might feel drawn to the scenic beauty of parks, gardens, rivers and lakes or to other displays of inspired art or simple elegance, while inwardly we must renew our trust in our primordial nature. We need to trust our longing for decency as a positive instinct. Bringing inner views and outer activities together means putting inspiration into action. When body and mind are synchronized, the present moment is a sacred fountain that recharges our confidence and uplifts our spirits.

An enlightened society can only be built on an accurate appreciation of reality. We can begin working with the setting sun by accepting that imbalance rules phenomenal existence. This means that the pendulum of despair can only swing so far in one direction before negative forces start to reverse themselves. In fact, as we approach the sunset we also approach the dawn. Thus we have to work with others. Like us, their spiritual imperative for survival has been fertilized by emotional and psychic suffering. Every year hundreds of thousands of individuals turn to mindfulness disciplines because they have had enough existential misery. They may not realize it, but they are driven to wakefulness by evolutionary instincts that are deep within us all. These inner forces are heightened at this time in reaction to events of the outer world.

Indeed, on some level, each of us is a pawn in Mother Nature's game. When we rise up to confront untenable conditions, we become like the floods, forest fires, earthquakes and droughts that we so often fear. Our voices join nature's chorus calling for balance. Each of our insignificant little chirps adds to the greater communal response. So, our spiritual reactions to the setting sun may start gathering momentum across the globe, and before long that evolutionary roar will be heard throughout the universe.

Because of nature's shifting inequities, we are caught in a continually churning flow of energy. Nothing in this universe is ever entirely inert: neither external objects, nor events, nor thoughts and certainly not our dreams. Therefore, we can never give up on life. At dawn, we go for a walk on the beach and the sea is peaceful and calm, yet by nightfall, a turbulent storm is thrashing the coastline. The soft summer mists hover over the silent morning valley, but before nightfall, that same gentle river swells into a rushing torrent filled by thundering rain. The finest tapestries and plushest carpets of the wealthiest mansions were woven by the poor, and one day they will be sold at a garage sale. Imbalance cannot be contained within balance; even though balance may be what imbalance strives to restore. Without this dance of disparity, existence as we know it would be essentially untenable.

Every action, even within our bodies, is performed as a reaction to some form of imbalance. We breathe in because we have breathed out and our lungs need oxygen. And then we breathe out because we are overloaded with carbon dioxide. We rise in the morning because we can no longer sleep; when our bladders are full they have to be emptied. Even the tiniest neurotransmitter surging across a microscopic synapse is an irresistible response to an imbalance internally felt or perceived. How could life function otherwise?

No form can endure. Things move forward through time propelled by the gravity of imperfection. We may believe we are muddling toward perfection, but the horizon of time keeps moving in front of us, splintering the status quo as it goes. Social, scientific, spiritual, and artistic revolutions are launched over and over as old ways of coping give birth to new ways of seeing. Even the ship of reason cannot linger long in the harbor of complacency. Floating quietly in some sheltered bay is not what the human intellect is built for. Powerful priests, mullahs and potentates often seem solidly entrenched six months before their regimes fall. No one can predict the future with 100% accuracy. All that is certain is that our current paradigm will splinter as new ideas emerge.

Monumental changes seem to happen very quickly in this modern era. It took millions of years to invent an abacus, then maybe a thousand more to improve upon it and create the slide rule. Today, a three year old laptop, already fifty times more powerful than the computers

used to put the first man on the moon, is considered quite
out-of-date. Our old ways of coping are dying and we
are giving birth to new ways of seeing at faster and faster
rates. Life, since beginingless time, has been one long
adjustment, and we are still fine tuning our instinctual
responses. Change is neither good nor bad, it is simply
the way things are.

Meditation allows us to glimpse the balance within
imbalance and the sacredness within the mundane. Just
as the horrors of war force us to seek new solutions to
old conflicts, setting sun claustrophobia pushes us to
extend beyond our cocoons. By probing the limits of
our awareness, we promote fresh and creative spiritual
instincts. When our dreams crumble, we suffer; yet when
our delusions collapse we are set free.

The forces of the Great Eastern Sun operate with primal
elegance. Every perceived imperfection occurs within the
sky of perfection. Only because things are falling apart
can we laugh, cry or ride the waves of joy and sorrow.
Without imbalance, dogs would never bark, birds would
never sing, minnows would never dart across the pond
and there would be no spring rains or autumn leaves. To
that end, the Great Eastern Sun teachings on Shambhala
warriorship have arrived at a critical juncture. Having
arisen in direct response to the degradation of the Setting
Sun, they have special relevance for us at this time.

20. Daring

From the first moment that we put any energy into the process of awakening, a remarkable transformation is set in motion.

A street magician in full banter demands of his audience, "Why be normal when you can be yourself?" The crowd of tourists and passers-by ripples with laughter. But even as they amble on and disperse into the summer heat, the question hangs in the air. What does it mean to "Be yourself"? After all, who else can you be?

In the conventional sense, we may think that we know who we are. We can list our likes and dislikes as well as our talents, strengths and weaknesses. Although perhaps embarrassed, we are not surprised by those predictable aspects of our personalities that surface at parties. On the whole, as model citizens and good *cocooners*, we're content to live within the confines of our habitual patterns and the rites and rituals of our tribe. Still, do we really know ourselves?

After all, a personality is not one single entity but a mysterious bundle of forces: memories, perceptions, defensive tendencies and millions of other factors. We have to accept that we are always a work in progress. At our funeral, friends and family may share some tender tears and amusement as they acknowledge their list of our closeted idiosyncrasies. But do they truly know us? Meanwhile, we may be slightly taken aback when a friend suggests that we have a few psychological blind spots. Often it takes a second to register that strange voice we hear on a tape recording as our own. If one

day our massage therapist diplomatically hints that
buried stress and unresolved conflicts may be causing
us health problems, we shrug in bewilderment. Yet, as
her skillful hands relieve the knots in our back and neck
and shoulders, we start to cry. What are these mysterious
obstructions and tangled energies? Where did they come
from and how long have they been here?

Generally, the narrow confines of our existence define the
only world we think possible. However, if we are lucky,
something happens in our lives that triggers spiritual
inquiry; we may encounter severe illness or death, suffer a
major loss, experience a dramatic change of fortune, have
a chance encounter with a sage, or undergo something
even more dramatic. Whatever the spark, when we
suddenly awaken, we are filled with curiosity. if they land
on the tinder of inquisitiveness, these sparks become fire
which, in turn, ignites further daring.

With our first step on the warrior's path a remarkable
inner transformation is set in motion. Whenever matter
moves between states energy is either released or
absorbed. As steam condenses into water or water freezes
into ice, energy is released. When ice thaws or water
evaporates, energy is absorbed. Likewise, as mind shifts
from cheerfulness to depression, we feel drained, and
when we move from depression and self-centeredness
to cheerfulness and spaciousness, we feel relief. It takes
energy to move away from ignorance and toward insight,
but as we do so, the mind starts expanding and our mood
lightens. Just as it takes a significant addition of energy
to transform a liquid to a vapor, breaking free of deeply
rooted mental habits requires daring.

The courage of daring has always played a major part in
the learning process. Think back to a time when you were
learning to swim or ride a bicycle. Can you recall how
daring was required? Can you remember feeling that

crescendo of fear before you let go and how good it felt when that energy finally gave way to a glowing sense of mastery? Removing the training wheels from your bicycle was daring. At the pool, holding your breath and floating for the first time was daring. Later, asking or accepting an invitation to dance with your latest crush was daring. Such challenges demanded that we harness our forces, face our fears and go forward. Despite the contractions in the pits of our stomachs, sometimes we needed to push through in order to let go.

Simply gathering courage and confidence, taking a deep breath and leaping into the space of nowness can be a matter of daring. Suddenly our horizons extend and the doors of freedom fly open. As soon as we recognize the familiar face of fear posing as the guardian at discovery's gates, we probably sense that we are going to need to arouse daring. The simple fact that we can acknowledge our trepidation, our laziness, our doubt or any habitual response, means we are already testing the cocoon. But in order to go further we must dare to question false assumptions, dare to shed our discursive thoughts and dare to step out of the swamp of habitual patterns. These little leaps become the footsteps on the path and mark the somewhat choiceless course of spiritual evolution.

Somehow, that day when we let go of our father's hand and did our first dog paddle or lifted both of our feet off the ground after guiding our little bike down a street, we set the stage for a empowering transformation. While maneuvering past any of these childhood milestones may have felt like a major achievement at the time, looking back, it all seems as natural as growing hair. For the fledgling warrior, breaking out of the cocoon is not always a dramatic event. Every day, subtle feats of daring go unnoticed; they blend into our days like a few raisins in a bowl of corn flakes. But over time, the results are truly monumental.

As beginning meditators, we tend to put a lot of energy into sitting practice hoping to reap immediate and tangible results. Initially, we may feel discouraged, but before too terribly long, discomfort and restlessness begin to settle and we savor our first real taste of meditation. Sitting practice is like putting a rosebud on the windowsill on a warm, sunny day. Nothing much seems to happen on the spot, or at least nothing we can discern with our ordinary senses. Yet, inside the cells of the rose, real changes are taking place. Somewhat dramatically, by the next day its petals have started to open. So it is with us. Once exposed to our own sanity, we start changing in ways that we can't explain. In a completely organic manner, a new lightness of being invades our smile, our conversation and our sex life. Because one day we dared to sit, all these changes feels quite natural.

I sometimes wonder what goes through the mind of a caterpillar as it approaches its cocooning phase. Does it feel old and wretched? Does it perceive that it is dying? Does it resist or naturally succumb to its growing fatigue? I expect nature has programmed caterpillars to resign themselves to the mysterious course of their life cycles. Still, after starting life as a furry little caterpillar, I can't imagine waking up one day as a monarch butterfly and not being a little surprised. When we look at the impermanence of our human form, we often are baffled by the ways our bodies and minds grow, age and change. We may try to cling to any one state of mind, one physical shape or one weight forever, but like caterpillars, we are involved in a process of continuous inner and outer transformation. Who knows, maybe we all have an inner monarch qualities just waiting to manifest!

Our genuineness cannot be indelibly linked to any one form. Presence is like a wave that continuously changes. It may surge and it may subside and shift and morph until maybe it hits the shoreline, but it never stops being part of the ocean. Being a wave, a caterpillar, a human body or a perfect warrior is always a work in progress within a context that is in continual flux. If we truly wish to know who we are, we have to dare to let go of any form or identity, and simply be. And in the end, daring to 'not know' sets us on a course of never-ending wonder.

21. Infinity

Through exposure to science, inner wisdom gains greater precision, and through exposure to spirituality, science gains hints of transcendence.

I love sailboats. The feeling of being on open sea, miles beyond the glow of civilization, is hard to describe. Give me a clear moonless night with waves lapping against a wooden hull and a mild but steady wind moving through the rigging and it won't be long before I am in bliss.

I doubt there's ever been a serious sailor, man woman or child, who has not imagined the life of an ancient mariner voyaging beyond the limits of the known world. Think of it! A gang of maybe fifty or sixty hearty men, a little lean after months of living on sea rations and stale water, all responding to a voice bellowing from the crow's nest, "Land! Land! Two points off the starboard bow!" It is easy to envision tired bodies coming to life, clamoring against a beaten rail and desperately straining to make out dim clusters of mist on a distant sun-baked horizon. I can almost feel their hearts beating out of their chests as those faint clouds transform into the peaks of Tahiti, Bora-Bora, Fiji or Tenerife, lifting their spent spirits into dreams of meat, fresh fruit, water, rum and fleshy adventures.

For me, one of the greatest joys of deep-sea sailing is that it provides a chance to be alone with my mind on the shores of the stellar universe. To be out on the water on a starry night, gazing into the depths of space, invites the dissolution of all the petty reference points of mundane life. However, a stroll along the beach of infinity today is quite different than it might have been for the salty midshipmen of Magellan, Cook or Columbus. Where they once saw constellations in the shapes of gargantuan beasts, reclining maidens and gods of war, I see planets, galaxies, thick bands of stars, billowing clouds of cosmic dust and a mind-boggling panorama of celestial events with overwhelming implications.

The heavens, as seen from Earth, have not changed all that much in the last five thousand years. Outer space has always been linked to notions of sacredness and divinity. When speaking of the 'Holy', the priest still glances skyward. Yet, from the pious Catholic to the total agnostic, no matter what humans believe or disbelieve, conceptual projections on infinity have never come close to containing what we behold in a clear night sky. Any curious human mind easily falls prey to the power of infinite stillness. We may be sophisticated enough to conceptually position the earth within a vast solar system and along one glistening spoke of a vast spiral Milky Way Galaxy, thousands of light years in breadth. Or we may be able to pick out the nebulous shapes of constellations that served our forebears as navigational reference points. Our modern view in no longer rooted in the myths of our ancestors; we have grown to see those same specks of light as distant suns and think in terms of vast spatial dimensions and distances measured in millions of light years. Primal awe, religious fervor, romance and speculation are all being recalibrated by refinements and advances in scientific knowledge.

One could say that science and spirituality are rocking forward like the port and starboard sides of the same hull. We might view infinity from the vantage point of either gunwale, but we'll always meet at the bow, which represents the crest of human understanding. As heart and mind come together, we are forced to bring the conceptual vastness of the intellectual universe and the ordinary magic of daily life into focus. Since Day One, scientists have been busily quantifying and extending our objectifyable outer experience, while, enlightened yogis have been refining the elixir of inner realization. Whenever these two disciplines merge, both are enriched. Through exposure to science, inner wisdom gains greater precision, and through exposure to spirituality, science gains hints of transcendence.

When a beam of white light is projected through a prism, it separates into a rainbow of different hues, each intriguingly beautiful. When the absolute is broken into facets of relative reality, each detail has truth and merit. One spark of clarity can illuminate a vast array of insights. We might study politics, psychology, carpentry, love affairs, finance or families, or veer into chemistry, biology, physics or epistemology, and find truths in all of these areas. But when a simple sailor looks deeply into the night sky, such complexity meets its nemesis. Efforts to establish a conceptual hold on the ultimate come up short. It is the nature of space to overflow whatever devices we use to contain it. Ultimately, vastness and emptiness are ungraspable by relative mind.

When we are caught up in a feud with our boss or waiting for a sandwich at the lunch counter, the enormity of space seems to be irrelevant. After all, what do distant galaxies have to do with the price of tomatoes? Actually, the vastness of the cosmos is not immaterial to our mundane existence. The infinite is inseparable from the finite. Space is the essence of everything- from the inside of tomato molecules to our emotional reaction at seeing how much they cost. It is only when we try to fit the universe into relative patterns of scale that we have trouble. The further we step back from the claustrophobia of our cocoons, the more the relative aspects of size, time and distances blend together like a play-within-a-play. As we step back further and further, our intellectual models of the universe expand and deflate like a cosmic bellows. One might think in terms of concentric waves emanating from a stone's plop in a still pond. An eighty-six foot wooden boat feels large compared to a tipsy canoe, yet tiny beside a massive cruise ship. What feels quite grand and stable in calm seas feels quite insignificant when tossed about by towering thirty or forty foot waves. One can see less than twenty miles from the poop deck of an average sailboat on flat water, making it necessary to refer to charts, globes and computer images in order to appreciate the magnitude of the oceans. We can barely grasp a sense of the curvature of the earth by looking at the horizon, yet by peeling an apple or a peach our minds can extrapolate that even the deepest seas are but a paper-thin skin stretched over this massive planet.

Our precious Earth, of course, is but a rare pebble within the immensity of our solar system. But this small family of planets and moons is merely our immediate sandbox; beyond it, millions of suns similar to our own share a much broader stellar neighborhood. Most of the stars that fill our visible night sky are part of our own galaxy, the colossal cloud of dust that we call the Milky Way. This relatively insignificant intersection of matter is, however, but a mere suburb in a vast intergalactic metropolis, which is, itself, considered minute within the larger nation of space. As our minds expand further, we may discover that our three-dimensional universe borders on other dimensions, with life forms that are currently inconceivable. Quite possibly, ours is only one of trillions of inhabited worlds. All the clusters of universes, galaxies, planets and the space between them may be nothing more than part of one small dust bunny in an otherwise empty sky.

If you are not already beginning to feel smaller than an atom within a mountain range, you are not keeping up. Ultimately, the limitless playground of conceptual speculation becomes its own graveyard. For if space is infinite, so is time. When we ponder the beginingless and endless nature of time, we experience an unsettling paradigm clash; we realize that whenever we look at anything, we are looking back in time. In the case of our cosmic horizon, what we see tonight will be an assortment of remnants of cosmic events from millions of centuries ago, thousands of centuries ago and last week, all lined up beside each other as if they had happened in the same time and space. In fact, all of eternity fits snugly into this one moment. The invention of time allows both the manifest and the unmanifest to partake equally in the unfolding miracle of creation. All the breaths ever breathed by any being on this or any other world, all the way back to the Big Bang and before, can be conceptually aligned within this present moment. Yet, it is only this current breath that is truly alive. Each cosmic event is just another note of the eternal waltz, making its impression and passing on as it transforms into another note. Sounds and vibrations may come and go but the music itself never stops, for the stillness includes everything.

Effectively, to be alive is to be a supernova in mid-explosion. Our momentary appreciations of space and time fold back into the infinite ocean of thoughts like waves splashing against the hull of a sailboat and blending back into the ocean. Even as our minds soar beyond our cosmic shoreline, we cannot leave this moment. Billions of neurons are streaming through microscopic synapses inside our brains and gallons of blood are being pumped through miles and miles of veins and blood vessels. All of this happens without a break from our birth to our death in order for us to sustain our miraculous bodies and process our thoughts. Several times very minute, our lungs inhale galaxies of microorganisms and expel hosts of others in the service of nature's grand ecological scheme. All the while, we are whirling through space at the speed of whimsy.

We are nestled into the nexus where the macrocosmic and the microcosmic coincide, where the organic and the inorganic, the past and the future and form and emptiness all momentarily share the spotlight. Here we are, and it is impossible to separate ourselves out from the whole, for in the space where relative and ultimate intersect, observer and observed are one.

22. Cheerfulness

Authentic cheerfulness gives fundamental sanity back its voice.

We all have carefree moments when we completely let go of our storylines. Somehow there is a natural lightness and simplicity to the occasion. We're in a good mood, actually a really good mood, and it doesn't particularly matter why.

My teacher, the Venerable Chogyam Trungpa Rinpoche, frequently implored his students to "Cheer up!" I don't think we were an unusually solemn lot, nor were we overly depressed. But, I remember feeling slightly perplexed by his entreaty until, fortunately, someone asked him precisely what he meant by "cheering up". His response was intriguing. *"Cheerfulness"*, he said *"means not holding anything in your mind"*!

I still find that particular answer illuminating. Of course, it is hard to be cheerful if we are obsessed, angry, holding a grudge or consumed by anguish. Cheerfulness, in the sense that Rinpoche was using the word, refers to a state of mind free of any agenda whatsoever. This kind of cheering up involves stepping back from the whole project of trying to 'do' life, in order to just 'be alive'. Essentially, Rinpoche's invitation to cheer up gave us permission to sit out a few laps of the mental rat race.

Setting aside our psychic loads opens up a carefree state of mind. Whatever we are doing, it is always good to stop and catch a conscious breath. It's not easy to step away from heightened emotions infused with a sense of urgency or to cut the ties to our more persistent narcissistic fixations, but when we do, we cheer up. In fact, cutting the flower of present mind from its gnarled stem and tangled roots demands fearlessness. This is what makes 'cheering up' such an interesting assignment.

Imagine trying to relate to a clear, open sky without being distracted, even as an intriguing wisp of cloud forms in the middle of the picture. Realistically, it is very hard to suspend all thought, even for a few seconds. It seems to be the nature of alertness that just as we become aware of the silence, some flicker of cognition steals our attention. According to the great meditative traditions, the skillful way to work with potential distractions is to touch any perception that arises and immediately let go! This light 'touch and go' approach is the essence of cheerfulness; like pressing the magic reset button that refreshes the world.

We may think of cheerfulness as a peak experience, the long-awaited fruition of a time-consuming and arduous process known affectionately as our 'spiritual journey'. But a simple moment of cheerfulness is usually much more spontaneous than that. Perhaps, all that happens is an accidental gap in our thought stream. It is as if we are engrossed in reading a newspaper when suddenly we smell burning toast. Although practice trains us to exploit these moments, we can't predict exactly how, when or why they might happen. Yet, suddenly we find ourselves in the midst of space. Maybe there's a kind of Murphy's Law that says we have to abandon all hope of a bull's-eye in order to hit the target. If we **try** to cheer up, nothing much happens, but when we relax, a smile forms.

As much as we have any choice in the matter, shifting our attitude and relaxing is an act of considerable kindness. When Trungpa Rinpoche invited us to 'Cheer up!' it seems that his intention was to inject some space into the claustrophobia of our own cocoons. Of course, he knew that a cheerful mind is fundamentally free; however, he was also asking us to extend ourselves for the benefit of others. Cheerfulness enhances and strengthens compassion. If we stop holding anything in our mind, even for a moment, the resulting mental state casts no shadow. When we are in a state of carefree, cheerful presence, our smiles become like the crystals on a chandelier, glistening with the rays of the Great Eastern Sun.

The epidemic of negativity and aggression plaguing contemporary society offers some insight into the importance of cheerfulness. Consider how negativity spreads in your life and in the lives of those around you. If you take a bath in the depression of someone close to you, your spirit can be dampened for days. Repeated interactions with chronically pessimistic or angry people can wound a childhood, derail a marriage or stunt a career. People surrounded by chronically bitter minds tend to become bitter themselves. Even certain forms of psychotherapy that revisit old grievances in the name of "self-exploration" backfire by reinforcing the seriousness and solidity of ego. When misinformed empathy empowers melancholy and cowardice, it may not be all that useful.

Fortunately, like negativity, cheerfulness is also contagious. Just as a depressed spirit can leave a noxious footprint, a truly cheerful outlook can open up the space and let in clean air and sunshine. One genuinely cheerful smile can spread throughout an entire subway car like a sneeze of delight. Authentic cheerfulness gives fundamental sanity back its voice. The subtle sighs or purrs that escape as we smell the lilacs blooming along the hedge loosen the stranglehold of self-absorption.

And when depression lifts, the basically good mind of cheerfulness is there like the fresh smell that follows a summer rain.

Everywhere we look we can see people with heavy issues weighing on their minds. Sometimes, life seems like a soup of grim, myopic, contagious concerns. Poverty, unemployment, a failing health care system and global warming, all these issues leave a trail of pessimism and atmospheric neuroses. So, rather than adding another voice to the chorus of apprehension, why not interrupt the flow of fear by coming back to the present moment? Actually, stopping the spread of aggression at the level of thought can be seen as the essence of socially responsible action. If we truly care about the mental suffering of others, we will feel compelled to reduce our negative emotional footprint! If not, regardless of our seemingly erudite political views or spiritual intentions, we are just another infected carrier of the plague of discontent.

Without cheerfulness to counter the bubonic forces of the setting sun, anxiety is bound to spread and depression will harden into more insidious forms of social unrest. So, in the spirit of fundamental sanity, let's take Trungpa Rinpoche's instructions to heart! Let's adjust our dial to the present moment, tune in to the underlying goodness of things as they are, and Cheer Up!

23. Bowing

Bowing is the practice of transcendental humbleness. Our intention is to surrender whatever gets in the way of genuine communication. Any lingering sense of façade is like a hat we remove when we extend a welcome.

Whenever people bow to each other, dignity should be part of the equation. Regrettably, in many cultures and particularly at this time, bowing is widely misunderstood. Bowing is seen purely as an extension of the politics of power and so sadly, this beautiful gesture has come to promote resentment.

A warrior's bow is a genuine expression of transcendence. An authentic bow is heartfelt and sincere. The hand is off the sword and the blade of impatience is set aside. Confusion and aggression are neutralized by elegance. Patience, vulnerability and alert, egoless attention are set out as a peace offering.

Watching an accomplished warrior bow can be subtly breathtaking. The bow begins from a dignified posture. If sitting, the back is straight and one assumes either a crossed-legged position or kneels so that the buttocks sit on the heels. If standing, one raises one's lungta and takes an upright stance with good head and shoulders. Sitting or standing, the hands are placed palms down at the top of the thighs with fingers pointing in and elbows curling outwards. In this posture, the arms are reminiscent of archery bows, bending as they are drawn. Wakefulness pervades the entire gesture and lends a sense of crispness.

Then with an attitude of heartfelt sadness, respect and confidence, the forehead slowly extends forward. Silently honoring the dignity of the present moment, first the head, then the body inclines. One offers up any sense of pride, arrogance or self-importance while, at the same time, offering a sense of richness. Head, shoulders, neck and torso are reminiscent of a flower with open petals leaning towards the sun. In extremely formal settings both hands would be placed on the floor in front making a small pad for the forehead. After a short pause at the bottom of the bow the head and shoulders unfurl. Like a flower drawing strength from the earth, the head is raised with a sense of renewal, and having tapped into the rich soil of primordial goodness, the body resumes its original posture in a state of presence without fanfare.

There are, of course, many forms of bowing, some very informal, some more elaborate, but the essence is always the same. Without expecting anything one gestures simply from the heart. A genuine bow can pacify the flames of disorder. The wind may be cold and the sky dark, the meal only half-cooked and the soup far too salty. Perhaps there is hair on the sink or someone has failed to keep his or her promise to walk the dog. Still, there is no reason to give in to a fit of annoyance. If inner dialogue invades a bow, the whole gesture loses power. Like pouring polluted water from a crystal decanter, something is incongruous; the sincerity of the bow is desecrated. An egoless bow reminds us that everyday chaos is fundamentally workable and even neurotic outbursts can be tamed. Whatever happens, a genuine bow stays rooted in basic goodness.

We have to accept mind as a work in progress. Without trying to make light of any turbulence, the practice of bowing simply looks toward the calmer water of simpler being where, ultimately, we accept gentleness rather than aggression as our baseline.

Of course, it is easy to be discouraged when bad things happen. It is common to hear complaints of how this or that teacher, politician or priest privately violates the very principles of decency they publicly espouse. We can expect this to happen from time to time, given that human beings are fallible creatures and that the forces of materialism are very strong at this time. It is difficult to maintain a sane and real connection with the warrior's world in the midst of a setting sun culture. But we should be careful in assuming that if someone is hypocritical or bigoted that he or she is not worthy of our bow. We might think that bowing to such a person would constitute surrendering our dignity to the setting sun. However, there are a myriad of faults in ourselves that would likely warrant us unworthy as well. So, in such a case, bowing is still worth the effort. For we bow not to the behavior, or to the words being uttered, but to the primordial goodness that may have been temporarily obscured. A genuine bow can cut through arrogance, our own as well as another's. If we bow with the intention of cultivating presence, hopefully some form of workability will emerge.

An authentic bow strikes a chord with everyone. Children bow with their ears when they hush to listen to crickets and frogs. An artist bows with a paintbrush as he or she touches it to the palette. The old man in the park bows to the ducks in the pond. Everyone bows to something. When we understand the power of bowing, we find ourselves secretly nodding to the goodness that is everywhere, and each time we raise our heads, our dignity radiates a little further.

Bowing is the practice of transcendental humbleness. Our intention is to surrender whatever gets in the way of genuine communication. Any lingering sense of façade is like a hat we remove when extending a welcome. An uncontrived bow is analogous to offering carefully prepared wholesome food on a beautiful silver platter. If the person offering and the actual gesture are not in harmony, both are diminished. When ego screams, "Notice ME, notice ME!" everyone feels very awkward; whereas, if ego is brought into check by a genuine bow, everyone sighs with relief. In due course, authentic warriors reach a point where every bow is satisfying. They never tire from bowing, just as they never tire from embracing virtue.

24. The Drala Principle

The hundred-year-old oak trees, the mosses, the waterfalls, and swamps all have much to teach us.

Regardless of where we are born, the culture of our upbringing or the circumstances we find ourselves in today, we are all subject to the same rules of nature. And like the laws that govern gravity or planetary motion, there are certain spiritual norms that transcend all religious ideals. It is a universal truth, for example, that resting in nowness is essential to wakefulness. Nowness is not the province of any one religion or philosophy but common ground shared by every genuine spiritual tradition. If we can drop our differences and inhabit the present moment, we can come together in an atmosphere of sacredness.

Whether we rely on meditation practice, prayer, contemplation, ritualistic dance, art or any egoless discipline is, in itself, not so important. The main point is to genuinely tune into the primordial stillness of being. When we fully enter into silence, we share the same mind. In the big picture, one silence fits all.

Over time, thousands of effective practices have emerged that people have found effective in their personal quest for realization. One might enter peace through arranging flowers, painting watercolors or walking in the mountains. We might be Sufi, Catholic or Agnostic; but if we are truly interested in waking up, sooner or later we return to silence. When the vast and the profound are contained in a raindrop, fewer words seem better. As our confidence strengthens, our access to the silence broadens and we stop filling space with unnecessary hubbub. Pauses become portals, and eventually, our whole world seems to be perforated with space.

As wakefulness seeps into the nooks and crannies of our daily lives, it is the ordinariness of things that strikes us as extraordinary. The simplest and most mundane events seem to be endowed with infinite possibilities. For the warrior at this stage, walking, speaking, making love- everything down to the simplest gesture- is seen as practice. Each moment presents a new opportunity to exploit coincidence and extend compassion.

Sakyong Mipham Rinpoche says, "A mind relaxed enough to appreciate the boundlessness of its inherent wisdom and compassion is no longer fooled into thinking that getting the best parking spot, winning every argument, or constantly finding faults in others is going to bring happiness." When we gain stability, the petty concerns of ego tend to evaporate like dreams at the end of a long night of sleep. Coming back to Square One is like opening our eyes to the familiar world we left the night before, minus the same old subplots and story lines. Instead of coming back to incessant complaints, we come home to spaciousness and sacredness. This is our real home-ground, the goodness that has no opposite. It is the space that both contains and fills the skies.

Sacredness inspires humbleness. If we are planning to meet a great teacher, we might dress up and greet their presence with the best mind we can muster. We might prepare an offering and even prostrate when we enter the room. But when the teacher appears in the form of the phenomenal world, we are caught with our pants down. Every breath is our bow, and this mind, with confusion and insight all mixed together, is our offering. When we see the world as a teacher, a profound sense of intimacy permeates the living universe. Such intimacy transcends our projections; it is a process best described as ordinary magic.

In this dance, our partners are what the Shambhala teachings refer to as *dralas*. The Tibetan word *'drala'* is often translated as *'wargod'*. Unfortunately, the term *'wargod'* may conjure up images of violence or superstition. Tibetans are primarily a nomadic and agrarian people, whose lives are closely bound to the elements. At times of conflict, warriors of various tribes and clans would draw on their deepest connections to the land and supplicate the spirits of their ancestry in order to rouse their confidence. They loved and revered their land, their yaks, their clouds and their mountains. If it was necessary to die in battle, they wanted to die feeling connected to the land and loyal to the dignity of their families, their lineages, or, at least to the three jewels.

However, the term *drala* goes far beyond rousing the courage for battle. *Drala* is also translated as *'above or beyond aggression'*. One Tibetan lama suggested to me that the word might have originated from a dialect that predates modern Tibetan. According to his explanation, *'Dra'* could be translated as *'voice'* and *'Lha'* as *'inner or higher'*. In this sense, drala could refer to the 'inner voice' of a place, situation or thing. To appreciate drala in this way, we need to listen to the world attentively with open ears, minds and hearts, free of projections or preconceptions. As we weave ourselves into the mystery from the macrocosmic to the microcosmic to the nanocosmic and back again, we learn to trust the magical forces that support us.

Human beings have always revered the natural world and all great cultures have had their dralas. Some were depicted in the forms of anthropomorphic deities or gods; some were said to reside in volcanoes or lakes; some ruled certain valleys or reefs, some are even said to manifest in the tips of arrows or fish-hooks. Regarding any object or location as a portal into the sacred world makes it worthy of veneration. Indigenous peoples from Polynesia to Tibet have had long standing relationships with power spots, medicinal plants, artistic themes and sacred landmarks. Rituals that highlight the vividness of this worldview fill the annals of human folklore as testimony to the pervasive role of the drala principle throughout the ages.

Today, much of the enchantment that enriched our past has been lost due to the skepticism of science. What once illuminated the human imagination is now disparaged as archaic or naive superstition. Yet, when we tune in to nowness, we still encounter the drala principle. Ancient civilizations and societies scorned as primitive and pantheistic actually produced architecture with more sophisticated resonance than our modern strip malls, office buildings, high schools or sports arenas. There are places in Europe where bridges built by ancient Romans survive to this day as wonderful examples of drala-inspired design. We have come to delight in the natural magnificence of certain structures, such as the Parthenon in Athens or India's Taj Mahal, that stand as testaments to the synchronized integrity of form and function. When artists or designers tune into the drala principle, they "catch a muse". That muse allows them to create objects of beauty endowed with something more than mere prettiness. The drala principle invites us to pay homage to the profound stillness of an uncluttered mind, and in so doing, rediscover sacredness.

America is a land of committed cynics. Still, cynicism can be humbled. Even the most jaded rationalists have been known to concede that the Grand Canyon, Yellowstone or Zion National Parks are home to something uniquely powerful. Much like the Tibetan warriors mentioned earlier, we turn to the natural majesty of our environment to inspire national pride and anchor our dignity. The beauty and power of certain rock formations, canyons, spectacular mountain vistas, turquoise lakes, geysers and other awe-inspiring phenomena are universally respected. The very creation of parks, in itself, is a custom with a powerful legacy rooted in the drala tradition. The Greeks, Romans, Egyptians and other great civilizations organized entire cities around their appreciation of dralas. Not just temples, and pyramids, but roads, bridges, waterways, fountains and arches had the power to inspire hints of a simple but elegant relationship between heaven, earth and man, that shimmered with transcendence.

The warrior's world is alive with dralas in the same way that the sky is alive with weather. Tuning in to the inner voices of things requires listening deftly to the elemental notes of the foreground, as well as the background, to the big, as well as to the small. Such listening begins with silencing discursive mind and letting go. We connect with the dralas not through ordinary thinking, not even with our ordinary ears, but with our hearts.

As a master warrior, Trungpa Rinpoche was always invoking dralas. One had the sense that he commanded a cosmic army that was always ready to support his efforts. Everything in his world had its place; every gesture had its elegance; every utterance had its meaning and its time. When he raised a glass of sake to his lips, it seemed as if he was sipping from a river of drala energy. When he walked into a crowded room, the sense of drala preceded him, and the power of his presence was quite palpable. When he sat in a chair, it became a throne of nowness in a court of precision and elegance.

A few years after his death, I attended a counseling seminar during which the instructor informed me that she had been present at one of Trungpa Rinpoche's lectures in Boston a number of years earlier. She was still struck by her initial impression. "All I remember was the way he walked into the hall." she said, "I felt as if the temperature in the room had suddenly changed. Things went hush and everyone's attention turned to this man who seemed to move with a kind of limp. It was impossible to take your eyes off of him. Everything around him sparkled. I remember remarking to my husband that I had never seen anyone enter a room so beautifully or with such command of the situation." {**Ed. note**: the left side of Rinpoche's body was paralyzed in a car accident, circa 1970}

Essentially, working with the drala principle demands that we develop a personal ecology of being. We may flirt with the conceptual frontiers of physics and mathematics but we cannot ignore our inquisitive hearts. We need sane and caring relationships with the earth and with the cosmos. Factual knowledge alone is not enough to sustain our evolutionary journey. The hundred-year-old oak trees, the mosses, the waterfalls, and swamps all have much to teach us. Their smells and textures contain more than we can glean from books alone. The farmer who bows to his garden at the end of the autumn and whose eyes twinkle at the sound of robins in spring has a different relationship to the earth than the scientist in a genetics laboratory. To understand the mechanics of change is one thing; to undergo a personal transformation is another.

What the dralas teach us is that wisdom finds expression in both light and in darkness. The voices of the dralas resonate deep within our DNA, and if we listen we can hear them. The dignified warrior, who knows the power of nowness, wisely relies on their guidance because reality is ultimately trustworthy.

25. Equanimity

Even a slight change of focus can break us out of our self-referential orbit and allow us to see things from a vaster, more awakened perspective.

Trungpa Rinpoche had an interesting relationship with time. In his world, the point was always to come back to Square One; thus, it was always now. If a talk scheduled for eight o'clock started at midnight, somehow it was precisely on cue. In his vast mind, conventional time mattered, but didn't matter. Precision was critical, but punctuality based on neurotic speed was less important. The only reference point that truly mattered was nowness. Whatever the occasion, Rinpoche remained unhurried and unhurriable.

The world of materialism is the domain of hope and fear. If we relate to time through the tainted lens of ego, we find ourselves either in a hurry or wishing things would slow down. It is with the same impatience that we project upon people the status of friend, enemy or stranger. When we are speedy, we are either for or against one another, or the people and events we are involved in simply don't matter. Likewise, when we operate on the basis of hope and fear, our mindfulness can be tainted with subtle forms of anxiety and our precision may be defiled by desperation. Meditation based on the hope that things will improve or the fear that they will get worse usually results in a self-fulfilling prophesy. If we are prone to such shallow practice, we are bound to lose interest and move on to the next ride, looking back at our 'spiritual period' with cynicism and scorn. All our classes in Buddhism and expensive weekend retreats will become just further episodes in a series of unfulfilled dreams and broken promises.

It is difficult to look closely at our own intoxication with hope and fear, especially if we are drunk on pride. Most of us are unaware that we are pervasively influenced by the eight worldly dharmas. Everything we do in the realm of ego, from the moment we open our eyes in the morning until the moment we close them at night, is motivated by at least one of these perverse and subtle forms of hope or fear. These eight include: *loss and gain, pleasure and pain, praise and blame, disgrace and fame.* Because of these eight, we are where we are today. Driven by the hope that this time things will be different and somehow better, all the while fearing that they may be worse, we get sucked in, again and again, like naive marks at some existential midway. Because of these eight, we will move from place to place, job to job, marriage to marriage and crisis to crisis following the same cycles of elation and despair throughout our lives. In effect, the wheel of samsara will continue to spin until we realize just how intoxicated we are by these eight persistent fixations.

The eight worldly dharmas provide the gravitational and centripetal forces that keep us enslaved by the sense of 'me'. Yet, even a slight change of focus can break us out of our self-referential orbit and allow us to see things from a vaster, more awakened perspective. For example, even attempting to shift from what Sakyong Mipham Rinpoche calls the 'me-plan' to the 'you-plan', might start to sober up an intoxicated narcissist.

The experience of freedom requires a full-blown paradigm shift. Maybe we live in the inner city and are subjected to a pervasive sense of hatred and hostility and develop a feeble identity replete with the low expectations and reinforced paranoias. Then, one day, something unexpected happens. We are suddenly transplanted to a rural community where people seem friendly and open. If we are hard-core city dwellers, such a move could be quite unsettling. When our new neighbors stop by just to welcome us to town or offer us baskets of food and vegetables from their gardens, we might not know how to react. In the streets of our old setting, suspicion and aggression kept us alive. Now, suddenly they seem to work against us.

Equanimity is a powerful tonic. It frees us from the patterns that have tied us in knots for eons by cutting through our neuroses. When equanimity dawns, we can reclaim our basic dignity. If our practice is strong, the seemingly irrepressible eight worldly dharmas are exposed for what they are: a cluster of narcissistic tendencies bound together by anxiety.

The dawning of equanimity can be like taking an airline flight on a rainy day. Imagine having to attend an important meeting in a distant city after a hard week. Stressed by the work and the tight schedule ahead, and having stayed up late the night before in preparation, you are already exhausted.

However, finally off and running, you start your car and begin wending your way through noisy traffic. You honk at slow cars or pedestrians crossing the street who insist on taking too long. When an unexpected detour threatens to add an additional eight minutes to your itinerary your sense of urgency ramps up and turns to rage. Looking at your watch, you smash your fist on the dashboard. How are you ever going to make it on time if traffic doesn't speed up? Anxiety levels surge at each clogged intersection. You veer in and out of passing lanes and charge through the yellow lights, pushing things to the limit. Each time you step on the accelerator, your thoughts speed up and soon you feel the rush of adrenalin join with your caffeine. You are almost out of control.

Miraculously, you arrive at the airport parking garage but with so little time to spare that you speed dangerously through the lot and rudely surge into the first available space. Grabbing your bag, you slam your car door and rush toward the terminal. Somewhere along the line, you start feeling like you have descended into a hell of hostility. There simply isn't enough time! Everyone is your enemy! On our way to the gate you hear the last call for your flight and have to sprint to make it through the boarding process just as the doors close.

Ten minutes later, however, the airplane pulls away from the gate and for the first time all morning, you can relax. Peering out at the runway you see fluorescent-vested baggage handlers with and rain gear waving their luminous wands. As the plane taxies down the concourse, watching other planes landing and taking off is fascinating. People look so small inside those little round windows.

After a few more minutes, your plane finally surges down the runway and you are thrown back against your seat. As it lifts its nose, you struggle to lean forward for one last look at the rapidly receding tarmac. As the plane gains altitude, the city below shrinks. Studying the patchwork patterns of grey streets and miniature buildings you are able to retrace your earlier route. There is the construction project that caused the detour. It hardly looks as stressful or as urgent as you rise above it all! It gives you a funny feeling to be able to view those boulevards and private gardens and cloistered backyards from our bird's eye view. What use are all those expensive fences and hedges now? You can see swimming pools, baseball diamonds, golf courses and the sprawling rooftops of shopping centers and factories. And, of course, there is your own tiny apartment building and the hospital, the church steeple and your favorite restaurant.

Ascending further, the whole metropolitan area disappears into a cloudbank. You have just enough time to adjust your seat and stretch your legs before your little capsule breaks through the ceiling of clouds and enters a world of endless, sparkling blue sky. Welcome to the upper atmosphere, where it's always a sunny day! Here, as if a huge weight has been lifted from your shoulders, you are again reminded that life with its traffic jams and neurotic relationships is only half the picture. No matter how hard it rains down below, regardless of your foul moods and urgent problems, the sun always shines above the clouds.

Being reminded that this wonderful earth quietly rotates on its axis and calmly abides in the midst of infinite space, lets us begin to appreciate how equanimity works. The universe is fine, just as it is, regardless of what some little scurrying ants might think. Reality is good. You might ponder a parting remark, or remember how it felt being caught in traffic, but in this moment, you are OK. You understand why people do many of the things they do and how those petty concerns affect you, but for now, it is time to relax into the vast sky of presence and enjoy your vantage point.

The Shambhala teachings speak of equanimity as the experience of *"Suddenly free from fixed mind"*. One moment we are absorbed in our projections of hope and fear; then, with an abrupt, purposeful shift of focus, we soar into the sky of equanimity. With one slash of the sword of *prajna,* the tight bonds of convoluted thinking are severed. Dropping the old paradigm of complaint and competition leaves us feeling unfettered and expansive. Having jettisoned the eight worldly concerns, we become like mythical garudas, whose equanimity is utterly free of hope and fear. The garuda symbolizes the warrior's dignity of 'Outrageousness'. Garudas bask in the vastness of the Great Eastern Sun, unaffected by narrow conventions or limited perspectives.

The outrageous warrior's dignified qualities are rooted in the expansive view of Big Mind. As we stretch our perspective to encompass an ever-widening horizon, the pettiness of ego becomes increasingly thinner and more transparent, allowing us to see reality with greater and greater accuracy. Rather than merely focusing on our own personal concerns, we start to think of those we love. Eventually, we extend our compassion to humanity as a whole. Then, surprisingly, we expand even further. Now our empathy encompasses animals and all other forms of life, seen and unseen, born and yet to be born, until nothing and no sentient being is exempt.

We understand that there is no time to waste on non-virtuous distractions or subtle resentments but also no purpose to self-condemnation or shame. We see that death is not the opposite of life but part and parcel of it. Equanimity transcends all forms of bias, including both optimism and pessimism. As it frees us of hope and fear we listen more intently, stay curious longer and watch the line between our friendships and our enemy-ships dissolve. No longer intoxicated with the eight worldly dharmas, we start to gain outrageous dignity in every aspect of our body, speech and mind.

In *The Dharma Bums*, Jack Kerouac shares a wonderful teaching on equanimity with his friend Japhy Ryder, (in real life, the poet Gary Snyder):

> *"...I run all my friends and relatives and enemies one by one in this, without entertaining any angers or gratitudes or anything, and I say, like 'Japhy Ryder,*

equally empty, equally to be loved, equally a coming Buddha,' then I run on, say to 'David O. Selznick, equally empty, equally to be loved, equally a coming Buddha,' though I don't use names like David O. Selznick, just people I know because when I say the words 'equally a coming Buddha' I want to be thinking of their eyes..."

I have found these three short lines (*equally nothing, equally to be loved, equally a coming Buddha*) to be very powerful objects of contemplation. I invite you to try using this prayer whenever you find yourself caught in a state of hatred, jealousy, passion or any other emotional mind. Go beyond yourself and your friends and try to include even those you regard as enemies. Take this prayer to heart as an experiment and observe what happens.

26.   First Thought, Best Thought

By relating to the world through the filters of second thought, we live in the wake of our original perceptions.

Usually the phrase "First-thought, Best-thought" warns us against over-thinking. In the context of making decisions, over-thinking can be very problematic. However, in the warrior tradition, "First-thought, Best-thought" takes on a slightly different tone. Here, 'First-thought' refers to the spark of wakefulness that ignites each perception, and 'Best-thought' points to the fact that 'First-thought' cannot be improved upon. So, in this context 'best' equals 'virginal', like the clear, pure water we find at the source of a river, and 'First-thought, Best-thought' refers to the non-dual immediacy that is the nature of awareness before neuroses have had any real chance to form.

In the iconography of Buddhist tantra, the principle of 'first thought' is depicted as a deity. As we look at artistic representations of tantric mandalas, our attention is drawn to the powerful dominant figure whose brilliance naturally radiates outward. Usually tantric deities brandish symbolic implements and sport adornments that represent aspects of wisdom and compassion, while the central deity herself or himself, personifies the essence of nowness: nondual, primordial presence.

'First-thought, Best-thought' is the primal scream of wisdom, the energy that bristles before the flame ignites. It happens so quickly that conceptualization seems slow and awkward by comparison. The words or mental images that we paste on top of immediate experience are actually second thoughts, third thoughts or tenth or twentieth thoughts. In Vajrayana Buddhism, techniques such as visualization, mantra recitation, mudras and energized contemplations are all simply tools for stabilizing and strengthening the practitioner's relationship with the freshness of first-thought.

Try, if you can, to step back and let thoughts arise and disperse without providing any commentary. Even though thoughts and concepts form like mist on a cold mirror, the nakedness of the mirror is always there first. Look intently and you may experience a figure-ground shift. What you see is not a patch of clear mirror in a sea of cloudiness but the other way around: the mists of thought are blotches in a sea of clarity. Look at your mind and see if you can shift your focus to the space in which thoughts form and into which they dissolve.

Staying present and simply observing thoughts arise, dwell and disperse leads us to the event horizon of mind's effervescence. Great meditators establish a seat on that precipice and basically mix their minds with space. They are able to rest in the luminosity of first thought experience without thinking about whether they are thinking.

By way of contrast, the central figure in our everyday lives, the mandala of confusion, is ego. We sense a big ME that draws its sustenance and solidity from the past, the future and even present conditions. This fumbling monolith presides over a loose hierarchy of thoughts, perceptions and emotions and conscripts all manner of mental and physical actions into its retinue. In fact, the role of the big ME is more like that of 'commentator' than 'player'. Ego functions a little like the voice-over when you are watching sports on T.V. Quite possibly, the athlete in the process of catching a pass or shooting a puck abides in the 'zone' of first-thought. For that person, in the rush of the moment, there is no need for commentary. However, for the fan on the sofa watching the game, the familiar voice of the announcer adds that little *'je ne sais quoi.'* Somehow the same catch is more 'real' with the embellishment of an excited disembodied voice yelling, "Touchdown!"

By relating to the world through the filters of second thought, we live in the wake of our original perceptions. Rather than engaging with the world from the bow of our boat, launching into new waves of freshness, we see the world from the stern. We may speak of living in the present, but we actually live in the immediate past. When we say things like: "Guess what, I just had a great idea!" or "Hmmm, a thought just occurred to me...!" we use the past tense. Ours is a world that has just happened, dragged down by our histories and skewed by projections. Whereas an enlightened person recognizes that thoughts have no composer, no owner, and no lasting form. Before ego rushes in to seal, copyright, patent or otherwise plant the flag of MINE on every thought that arises, the event is over. There is no desire to own every square inch of intellectual property that we happen upon and claim it in the name of the empire.

Thoughts are transient and elusive; they are not dictates from heaven nor are they the voice of perfect reason. Ironically, if we try to stop thinking, we can't! And conversely, if we try to hold on to a thought, it slips away. So, the message of 'First thought, Best thought' is to be totally straightforward and appreciate the freshness of each moment by letting reality stand on its own.

27. Elegant Speech

The art of simple and clear communication is going the way of polar bears and glaciers. Not only are we witnessing the desecration of plants, animals and birds, but we are losing our poetry as well.

Although born and raised in a remote corner of Tibet, once Chogyam Trungpa Rinpoche was forced to flee his homeland he took to the English language like a gifted musician picking up a prized violin. He listened closely to the way his students spoke and, at some point, lamented their casual disregard for the beauty and power of their own voices. He encouraged us to re-examine the words and phrases we used along with the intentionality behind their use. Noting that the proper use of any language is inconsistent with deceit, dishonesty or slander, he encouraged us to taste each word or phrase and savor it like a nutritious morsel in a tasty stew. He exalted in the subtleties of meaning, appropriate humor and elegant dialogue and delighted in the candlepower of poetry. Trying valiantly to nurture a healthy regard for proper diction in a culture raised on slang, he seduced subtle nuances out of common words until everyday phrases sparkled with newfound clarity.

During formal talks, Rinpoche would regularly stop speaking to sip a glass of water or saki. Those pauses were memorable and transformative. He would look at his glass, slowly extend his arm and pick it up, take a sip and replace it on the side table. Something within that simple gesture opened a portal into a more refined vibrational plane. Such sips of silence provided more than punctuation; they perforated the minds of the audience and added a natural elegance to his speech. Since he was never rushed by mental speed, each word was afforded just enough space to release its full fragrance.

Because he always seemed to be rooted in the present moment, his words always had the multidimensional eloquence of beautifully uttered dharma. That immoveable feeling of centeredness, of genuine presence and confidence devoid of aggression, could be more than a little intimidating. Yet, it was always refreshing. Even if those in his company were frantic or falling asleep, the air around him set the standard for brilliant sanity and the aroma of fresh insights often wafted throughout the room like incense.

Whether in verbal or written form, communications with Rinpoche were never entirely casual. Every note, gesture, comma, smile, frown or nod had its own specific gravity. Every conversation, no matter how brief, was a teaching. His message was not sugar-coated or even necessarily pleasant, but if you approached with a receptive mind, your world was sure to be illuminated. Likewise, if you approached with uptightness or anger, those sentiments were reflected and often amplified in an atmosphere of spaciousness. Observing how words and space could become the raw materials of transmission was always edifying. Such is the nature of pure speech.

Despite the fact that he could go days without saying more than a few words, Rinpoche was a master conversationalist. We used to joke that it took about twenty seconds for Rinpoche to get to know someone completely. At a dinner with a few of his students, a subject might be introduced only to be set aside for a few moments. As the flow of dialogue drifted in a different direction, one was left floating in subtle anticipation. Then, after being left to steep just long enough for the mix of flavors or ideas to reach full potency, Rinpoche would return to the theme and add a simple comment, sparking a whole new round of epiphanies. He took great enjoyment in drawing out the natural wisdom of the situation.

Padmasambhava, the great 9th century Buddhist master, once said, *"When alone, one should guard one's mind. When with others, one should guard one's speech."* This point was quietly hammered home in the company of Trungpa Rinpoche. Verbal sloppiness, slander or grammatical slurs could leave one feeling as awkward as if one had just passed gas. Mindfulness of speech can have a profound effect on the mind. Paying attention, not only to the words we use, but also to the silences between the words, can change the tones and cadence of our utterance. In Rinpoche's presence, instead of feasting on ideas and clever verbal remarks, space itself became the main course. Sharing the most brilliant insights seemed almost gross, like stating the obvious. Holding one's tongue was the equivalent of holding one's seat. When the mind was allowed to come to rest, all words might evaporate leaving one suspended in the refined embrace of reality. As thoughts vanished into non-thought, only the most essential vowels and consonants of immediacy would remain.

Dinner parties at his residence, the Kalapa Court, would frequently transform into spontaneous literary events marked by the composition of poems. Guests were not only expected to dress well, they were expected to speak elegantly. He was, after all, training us to be dignified warriors with good manners, capable of grace, creativity and verbal elegance. Celebrations, such as the Tibetan New Year (known as Shambhala Day), were particularly sumptuous affairs. All would don their Sunday finest; the mood was always very uplifted and the company, splendid. The idea was to create a living example of enlightened society: gracious, full of humor, elegant, dignified and truly enjoyable. And, of course, mindfulness of speech was always "de rigueur".

I remember being with Rinpoche and a small group of students in an apartment in New York City. It was a late spring afternoon and a senior aide, charged with an important administrative post, seemed to be constantly on the telephone. As this fellow paced back and forth in the kitchen, segments of his long distance phone conversations would intermittently trickle into earshot of the group assembled with Rinpoche in the living room. The ceaseless rise and fall of his strident voice highlighted and extended the gaps in our own discussion. It had long become apparent that when there was nothing to say in the presence of the guru, it was best to say nothing. At one point Rinpoche smiled and said, with a twinkle in his eye, "Wouldn't it be interesting if, when you were born, you were issued a certain number of words? And when you finished using them all, you died?"

As an aspect of Shambhala decorum, Rinpoche introduced the practice of elocution in the mid 1980's. He had decided that it was time for his English speaking students to learn to speak their language properly, without 'Americanisms". People initially nonplussed by this new and challenging practice were tempted to dismiss it as a kind of quaint parlor game or as one of Rinpoche's idiosyncrasies. It soon became clear, however, that this was no joke. The challenging practice of honing our speech patterns revealed just how neurotic and mindless our use of language had become.

A typical elocution lesson would begin after a late discourse on a Buddhist or Shambhalian topic. Rinpoche would have microphones strategically placed around the hall and ask for volunteers. Following his example, several brave martyrs were instructed to repeat short phrases or sequences of phrases, paying keen attention to cadence, tone and clarity. Rinpoche would usually begin with a phrase like:

Rinpoche: "Kathy's hair is black!"

Student: "Kaatheeze hayer is Blaack!"

Rinpoche: "Not quite it, I'm afraid. Try again...
Kathy's HAIR is BLACK!"

Student: "Kathyzz HHAAIRR is BLAck."

Rinpoche: "Hmmm. "Better, but not quite. Once
more, listen closely...
Kathy's HAIR,... HAIR... HAIR... is BLACK!"

And so on. For what seemed like an eternity, three to
four hundred people would sit patiently listening to
Rinpoche's victims stress a syllable or experiment with
inflection. Finally, they would arrive at a true rendition
and everyone would sigh with relief. At which point
Rinpoche would mercifully move on to the next line:

Rinpoche: "Her complexion is white!"

I remember squirming as my comrades fell on their
swords uttering these seemingly meaningless but
complicated phrases. Yet, to everyone's amazement, the
exercise had a penetrating and profound effect. For days
after an elocution lesson the world of speech would feel
slightly altered. Not only were we more aware of vowels
and consonants, but we tuned in to the songs of birds
and even the drones of air conditioners. I remember
becoming much more aware of the musak on an elevator
and the roars of distant airplanes. Even in conversations
with strangers, the tone, meaning, cadence, volume, and
in particular, the correct pronunciation of words, all fell
under silent scrutiny.

Sadly, such training is rare. Today, perhaps more than ever, elegant speech seems to have entered a phase of accelerated decline. The average person takes their use of language utterly for granted. Indeed, as further evidence of this Setting Sun era, the art of simple and clear communication is going the way of polar bears and glaciers. Not only are we witnessing the desecration of plants, animals and birds, but we are losing our poetry as well.

The decline of eloquence coupled with an increase in public and political slander has left us vulnerable to many forms of devastating cultural decay. As it is, crass sloppiness on a level that would have been totally unacceptable to the average citizen a century ago, has crept into common parlance. Much of the vitriolic ranting that passes for political commentary would never have been tolerated in respectable societies of the past. But perhaps the most unfortunate aspect of this development is that no one seems to care.

In what proved to be the twilight of his teaching career, Trungpa Rinpoche's style of presentation underwent a subtle shift. His talks became shorter, the cadence of his speech gradually slowed, and the gaps between his words seemed more elongated. The tempo of activity around him also changed. It might be tempting to attribute all of this to physical aging or to some loss of acuity, but in his case, these adjustments were haunting manifestations of skillfulness. An even clearer and more potent sense of presence pervaded every action and utterance. His relaxation into space allowed an even more subtle sense of humor, inner peace and stillness to shine through. Opportunities to be with him were more precious than ever before. When Rinpoche died in 1987, he was considered relatively young, but if he used up all his words, he didn't waste any. His legacy of sacred utterance still echoes with profundity and for those who listen, his presence still echoes in the dangling silence at the end of thought.

28. Courtship

When ordinary language slips into the mouths of lovers,
it becomes a kind of sacred music.

As an expression of primordial basic goodness, Great Eastern Sun vision is nothing new. Those civilizations that have aspired to uplift their societies on the basis of distilled visions of basic human dignity have become inspirational to those that followed. In the Imperial Courts of medieval Japan, for example, the standards of elegance and sophistication that informed almost every aspect of daily existence have left an indelible footprint on our modern era in areas of art, cuisine, architecture and military decorum. We are aware that people of that time had a deeply embedded tradition of bowing, and if we can trust the surviving poems passed between courtiers, it seems elegant speech clearly signified respectability. Certain examples of exchanges between gifted young courtiers are breathtaking for their gentleness and attention to detail as well as for their spacious, natural simplicity.

Imagine the atmosphere of an aristocratic estate where political and family alliances extended across generations. Casual liaisons graduated from mere social pleasantries into bonds that could span lifetimes, often on the basis of carefully composed poetic exchanges. Structured and formal social contacts may have been mirrored in more structured verse, while more intimate associations gave birth to the haiku (three-line) or waka (five or seven-line) style marked by simplicity, economy and intrigue. These beautifully-crafted short verses provide unique glimpses into human nature by drawing on images of the natural world.

Words skillfully and tenderly used can carve peepholes into the sacred world. One image or line of verse shared between lovers might be savored for a lifetime. The right combination of syllables can trigger a discrete mutual celebration of a fleeting sunrise or highlight the sad and tender poignancy of an autumn leaf on wet grass. Because of the range of graceful effects human beings can have on one another, delicacy of expression is treasured as a sensual art form.

Nothing can energize the world of love, sexuality and courtship like an intimate poetic exchange between suitors. Within the refined cultural container of the Japanese court, spirituality and social survival were often mutually entwined. Composing a poem involved more than simply jotting down a few words on a page, it invoked the sophisticated art of calligraphy. As much might be communicated by how syllables were executed on the page as by their meanings alone. Each stroke of the brush revealed an aspect of the communicator and little nuances were seldom intended to go unnoticed.

Thus, the art of dignified communication involved knowing how to hold a brush and how to execute an elegant stroke, along with all that such talents entail. An educated courtesan would be expected to have a basic knowledge of inks and papers and be cognizant of the etiquette surrounding the placing of a personal stamp or seal. But more importantly, the entire exercise lent itself to introspection. Since poetry is grounded in perception and since seeing requires taking the time to notice details, speed was not considered a virtue. Appreciation takes time. Too rapid a response would have suggested a lack of refinement. Just as it could take several hours to bathe and dress in a formal kimono, or take more than an hour to rake a rock garden, it took time to digest and respond to a poetic missive. Factored into such activities was the

time required to cultivate mindfulness and awareness
and come to know oneself.

In the dignified society of an Imperial court, much as in
any society, true depth of character implied keen personal
observation and introspection skills. The acquisition
of social graces was subtly intertwined with a deep
appreciation of the past combined with a genuine sense
of presence. For a young warrior, each new situation
presented a canvas on which to exhibit confidence and
originality, but it helped to have a grasp of the styles
and skills of the great poetic sages. In particular, young
warriors in love who dared to imitate particularly well-
known calligraphy masters would have to balance
bravado with appropriate humility. A callous or coarse
reference might betray a flaw in one's character or a leak
in one's integrity. Likewise, the freshness of the moment
might call for a certain ink or a carefully chosen paper,
neither too shiny nor too pale. With just the right amount
of pressure and the perfect nonchalance of sway in the
brush, and with a subtle flare or innuendo at the end of a
down-stroke, a disciplined but passionate heart was laid
bare. Once attracted by these petals of subtlety, what bee
could resist such a fragrance?

Over the course of a day, youthful minds would absorb
impressions like the papers on which love poems were
composed. While she was secretly and wistfully plotting
to have a scroll delivered to her lover's quarters at a
precisely chosen hour, he would be gazing at dragonflies
and stalks of bamboo beside a garden pond. Each would
be searching for just the right nuance. A particular bird
might warble in the evening just as the first lanterns were
lit. How can a bird's song broadcast the most intimate of
feelings and not be poetic? If, as the late autumn shadows
shimmered across the silvery surface of the lagoon
a stealthy messenger cautiously appeared at a door,

should she be preceded by a faint but certain scent? The handmaiden would be carefully instructed. She was to drop off a scroll as if her delivery were merely a casual, unrehearsed errand at the end of the day and then linger to observe his reaction. He, of course, would be entirely gracious and invite the handmaiden to wait just a moment while he jotted off a spontaneous reply. Of course, such spontaneity had been gone over a thousand times in his mind during a full day of contemplation. Nonetheless, in the spur of the moment he just might surprise even himself.

Any messenger chosen for a role in this secret communication would consider it a quiet honor, as simply being privy to such intimacy was an indication of exceptional trust. Of course, the handmaiden or the gentleman's manservant would vicariously enjoy the dance almost as much as the young courtiers they served. The performance of such duties might require her to imitate his lordship's expression by raising her eyebrows, or he to suggest the softening of the expression on her ladyship's face by swooning and hiding behind a fan. And of course, as each of the intended opened their respective scrolls, they knew that their reactions would be reported. Those most skilled in such arts would find ways to use whatever might be available to unfurl the exquisite lotus petals of intimacy.

Both lovers would undoubtedly be aware of the current phase of the moon and the flowers that were in season, for if they could not share each other, at least they could revel in the same moonlight and know where and when the best blossoms could be viewed. They might delight in noting at what hour the migrating birds were expected to appear. Such ordinary observations highlighted meaningful events, suggesting to both the vastness of a world beyond their own and a passionate intimacy just beyond their grasp.

When ordinary language slips into the mouths of lovers, it becomes a kind of sacred music. Well-trained words assigned to express the innermost secrets of a sad and tender heart become the most sensitive and resourceful of servants. When a poem enlists atmospheric silence, each phrase becomes a natural and unconfined portal into the sublime. Of course, the spontaneity of first thought is necessary to keep things fresh, for if too much care is spent planning exactly how, when, and where to place a particular letter on a page, the whole poem becomes awkward and clunky. One might think the poor, love-struck poet was involved in planning a bank robbery.

But so much for ancient Japan! Let's imagine ourselves in this scenario. What role does love play in our communication with the world? Can we see that our words and gestures are only intermediaries, that it is because of love, itself, that we notice the blue flax flowers? Of course, the tall reeds and stalks of pussy-willow were already there, but until the lover inside us points them out, they go largely unseen. Alas, the lake is here, the moon is here, and the waves are lapping against the shore even as we speak. Perhaps it is the end of a short summer. Quite soon the leaves will change and the pumpkins will ripen. The phenomenal world is just outside the window, serenading us in coded dialect. Perhaps it is love that makes us listen more closely. Let's be quiet so our hearts can hear.

Attention is the handmaiden, the manservant and the message. Furthermore, the one sending us such delicate haiku is not an actual person, but the magic of presence itself. Let's calm our minds, pay attention and listen. Let's fill our nostrils with the tantalizing air of unconditional love that transcends even the most fundamental aloneness. What lover could possibly be more powerful and provocative than this present moment?

If we are prepared to enter a love affair with reality, the beauty and richness of life is poised and ready to meet us. We need only embrace nowness with all our hearts. If we open the morning curtains with unrequited passion or kneel privately by a waterfall, the immediate world will grant us access to the inner court of sacredness. Every sound, every gust and every taste of every drop of rain will be utterly sincere. The shadow of the passing cloud moving over the abandoned soccer field is a poem written only for you.

When we fall out of love with the world, we need to rouse our lungta and express ourselves as poet warriors. Whether we are greeting a colleague, a client or our date for the evening, we can take a moment to breathe between our sentences and summon the best of our attention. If we can drop our own fixations with ourselves, we will probably notice the quality of their eyes and feel their confusion or sadness. Once we can bow and offer our own presence with genuine care and fearless attention, we can again be meek, humble and cheerful companions. Our minds may wander, but the world never abandons us. Once we have been invited to participate in the sumptuous feast of eternal doubtlessness, there is no turning back.

The blessings of this moment, this now, right now, are ours to give and receive. When we open to our tender hearts of sadness we find they are wet with life and tinged with sacred fondness. The true nature of love is nowness. And since we are never separated from this very moment, love pervades all of space. Listen and you will hear it. Open your eyes and you will see. Open your heart and mind and the dignity of the Great East will illuminate your way.

Good luck to you! Good luck to us all!

Thank you for reading

To order more copies of this book, or to order it in an iBook or electronic format, Please see the author's website at:

http://www.listeningmind.org/

Also, for more information about Shambhala teachings or programs, the following links may be helpful :

www.shambhala.org/

www.karmecholing.org/

www.shambhalamountain.org/

Regarding *The Ven. Chogyam Trungpa Rinpoche*

www.chronicleproject.com/

http://oceanofdharma.com.

Regarding *Sakyong Mipham Rinpoche*

www.mipham.com/

Breinigsville, PA USA
11 April 2010
235902BV00001B/4/P